ORGANIZATIONAL GRAVITY

*A Guide to Strategically Growing
Your Company's Brand, Culture, and
Talent*

TONY KUBICA AND SARA LAFOREST

TABLE OF CONTENTS

PREFACE   xi

INTRODUCTION What Is Organizational Gravity?   xiii

PART ONE: BUSINESS GROWTH STRATEGY

CHAPTER 1   Business Growth Strategy   1

CHAPTER 2   Business Growth Strategy Supplement: A Series
             of Tips and Techniques to Help with Strategy
             Formulation and Guidance   13

  • *Strategic Planning*   *13*
    o Setting Direction and Taking Action   15
    o Defining Your Strategic Core Statement   17

  • *Creating a Strategic Vision—Are You Making the
    Three Mistakes Most Organizations Unknowingly
    Make?*   *19*
    o Understanding How the Marketplace
       Impacts You   21

  • *Implementing Your Strategic Directives: Don't Be
    One of the Many Failed Plans*   *23*

  • *Is Your Success Your Biggest Problem?*   *26*
    o Complacency in Strategy Can Ruin Your
       Business   27
    o An Absence of Business Common Sense   29

  • *The Business Basics: You Can't Succeed without
    Them*   *31*

  • *Evidence-Based Business Growth*   *32*

  • *Beware the Business Inflection Point*   *34*
    o Getting Beyond the "Pain Point"   36

- *Growing an Imperfect Business: Go for Success, Not Perfection*   *38*
- *Aligning Your Executive Team*   *40*
- *The Knowing–Doing Gap: A Competitive Edge*   *41*

PART TWO: BRANDING

CHAPTER 3   Branding   45

CHAPTER 4   Branding Supplement: A Series of Tips and Techniques to Drive Brand Building   55

- *Is Branding Really Worth it?*   *55*
- *Seven Questions to Help Build Your Brand*   *56*
- *Branding Starts with Identifying Your Target Market*   *57*
- *Building Your Brand Identity*   *61*
- *Differentiation Is Not Doing What Everyone Else Is Doing*   *63*
- *The Risk and Commonality of Brand Ambiguity*   *65*
- *Protecting Your Brand*   *68*
- *The Placebo Effect and Your Business*   *70*
- *Are You Managing Your Company's Reputation? Avoid Damage Control*   *71*

PART THREE: CULTURE

CHAPTER 5   Culture   77

CHAPTER 6   Culture Supplement: A Series of Tips and Techniques to Foster Culture Building   91

- *Culture and Brand – The Bedrock of Business Growth*   *91*
  - o   Creating the Promise – Your Brand   92
  - o   Creating the Culture to Deliver the Promise   93
- *Consistency Builds Culture and Enables Growth*   *95*
- *Culture—Made by Intention and Filled with Stories*   *97*

- *The Power in Words*   *99*
- *The Language of Business*   *102*
- *Metaphor for Culture: The Atom and the Organization*   *103*
  - o   The Unsung Hero   105
- *Are You Supporting the "Shadow" Organization?*   *106*
- *Avert a Culture of Complacency*   *108*
- *Healthy Conflict*   *110*
- *Driving Innovation*   *112*
- *Tribalism*   *114*
- *The Value of Values Alignment*   *117*
- *The Happiness Link to Better Performance*   *119*
- *Culture and Emotional Equity*   *120*
- *Managing the Gap between Your Actual Culture and Your Intended Culture*   *121*

PART FOUR: PROGRESSIVE TALENT MANAGEMENT

CHAPTER 7	Progressive Talent Management	125
CHAPTER 8	Talent Management Supplement: A Series of Tips and Techniques to Drive Progressive Talent Management	139

- *Talent Recruiting and Integration – Four Primers that Create Success*   *139*
- *Intelligent Selection Leads Talent Integration*   *141*
- *Internal Talent Recruiting and Integration*   *143*
- *External Recruiting*   *144*
- *Hiring for Fast-Growing Departments or Companies*   *146*
- *On Hiring*   *149*
  - o   The Perfect Fit Is Rare   149
  - o   How to Decide Who You Need   151
- *On Transitions*   *152*
  - o   When You Are the New Hire   152

    o   Five Ideas to Help with Your Move to
        Management   153

    o   What Can You Do as a Newly Appointed Manager
        to Establish Credibility?   155

    o   Transitioning Middle Managers   156

    • *Talent Management: How to Retain Top Talent
       Without Derailing the Organization when Fast-
       Tracking*   *159*

CLOSING

CHAPTER 9   Putting It All Together   165

BONUS SECTION   175

LEADERSHIP   177

    • *Leadership for Organizational Gravity*   *177*

    • *Leadership Qualities/Qualifications: One
       Debate That's Irrelevant*   *179*

    • *Leadership Starts from Within*   *180*

    • *Leadership: Closing the Learning-Performing
       Gap*   *182*

    • *Your Personal Energy Impacts Your Leadership*   *183*

    • *A Note on Executive Presence (Impression
       Management)*   *184*

    • *Oh, You Mean We Have to Do It? Accountability
       Matters*   *186*

    o   Accountability – A Growth Factor   188

    o   Five Prerequisites in Employee
        Performance Accountability   189

    • *Mid-Level Managers: Remember – Most
       Employees Leave Their Bosses Not Their
       Companies*   *191*

    • *"But" Deteriorates Performance*   *193*

    • *Building Your Emotional IQ to Improve Your
       Employees' Performance*   *194*

    • *Gratitude Has a Return*   *196*

- *Motivated, Aligned, and Satisfied Employees Are a Differentiator*   *197*
- *The "Undiscussables"*   *199*
- *Trust: Mirror, Mirror, on the Wall...*   *201*
- *A Leader's Edge: Influence without Positional Authority*   *204*
  - o   Influence is a Leadership Quality and a Management Skill   205
  - o   Enablers and Disablers in Influence   206
  - o   Influencing Strategies   209
- *Innovation – The Key to Reinvention and Reinforcing an Entrepreneurial Mood in Your Business*   *213*

A REMARKABLE COMPANY HEARS THE VOICE OF THE CUSTOMER   215

SUCCESSION READINESS FOR BUSINESS GROWTH AND CONTINUITY   219

WHY START YOUR EXIT PLANNING NOW?   226

APPENDIX

ORGANIZATIONAL GRAVITY ASSESSMENT   231

REFERENCES AND NOTES   239

ACKNOWLEDGEMENTS   245

COMPANY BIOGRAPHY   247

Dedication:

To entrepreneurs and business leaders committed to growing their companies and being remarkable. To your success!

PREFACE

The reason we wrote *Organizational Gravity* is to create awareness to help entrepreneurs and small business owners examine what it takes to build and grow a business.

Too often we find business owners, or would-be business owners, believing that if they just had a good idea for a product or service and adequate capital to get their business growing, the rest will take care of itself. Or perhaps they don't reflect on it quite this way, but they do believe growing a business would be relatively easy. None of this is true.

Anyone who has tried knows what we mean.

What we believe has been missing is the awareness that to grow a business successfully, four elements must be addressed—together:

1. A good and executable strategy
2. A brand that communicates your promise to the buyer
3. A culture that is designed to deliver on your promise
4. The talent required to execute effectively and competently on points one through three above.

In *Organizational Gravity* we provide a brief framing Chapter on each of the four elements. Accompanying each Chapter is supplemental reading that is intended to provide a short presentation of ideas that expands on the concepts presented in the Chapters.

What you will learn is why it is so important to connect strategy, brand, culture and talent.

As you read the book, you may wonder about specific areas such as sales, marketing, finance, human resources, IT, and other areas required to grow a business. Our belief is that other books have done an exceptionally good job developing these specific areas.

What we believe has been missing is the position that businesses are not just about sales or finance or any one skill. Businesses are about:

- whether you can develop an executable strategy that's relevant to your market and to your capabilities
- whether you can define a brand and a brand promise that is distinguishable from your competitors'
- whether you can build a culture that focuses on delivering on the brand promise
- whether you can acquire, develop, retain, and promote the talent required to achieve the above.

And yes, a good sales engine is necessary, along with strong financial resources, human resources, and IT skills. But they must be present within a gravitational organization if the business is going to differentiate itself from others and grow in the marketplace.

Small businesses today are in a much better position than they have ever been. They are in a great position to compete effectively with their much larger counterparts. Communication with buyers is almost cost free, and interconnectedness allows for a greater ability to find talent, resources, and support. Small businesses can be more creative and innovative and are clearly able to move faster from idea to offerings.

The move to the era of connectedness is here, which presents an unprecedented opportunity for the creation, growth, and success of the small business.

Tony Kubica   Sara LaForest
East Greenwich, RI   Arroyo Grande, CA
May 2013   May 2013

INTRODUCTION

WHAT IS ORGANIZATIONAL GRAVITY?

A resurgence in small business growth is critical for economic and job growth in this country. Signs point to improvement; but we have a ways to go. Not only do we need to see an increase in start-ups, we need to see growth in existing small businesses.

This book focuses on helping entrepreneurs, small business owners, and executives grow their businesses using a concept we call "organizational gravity." Organizational gravity draws both talent (employees) and customers to your business. And it does this through capitalizing on the interrelationship of strategy, brand, culture, and talent.

We, the authors, place a strong emphasis on attracting and retaining the right talent. Because ultimately, it's people who get work done. We believe to attract and retain the right talent you must have a compelling business model, a strong brand, and an effective performance-based culture. We take a people-centric approach to growth; not in isolation of strategy, brand, and culture, but as a key *enabler* to support your strategy, brand, and culture.

THE METAPHOR OF ORGANIZATIONAL GRAVITY

We know from high-school physics that bodies attract with a force proportional to their mass. Likewise in business, companies attract talent (and customers) with a force proportional to their organizational mass.

The mass in a gravitational organization[1] is a business growth strategy, a strong brand, a strong culture, and talented employees. And the greater the mass (strategy, brand, culture, and talent), the stronger the force is to attract and retain talent and customers, who are the lifeblood of the company. Talented people are essential to deliver on the brand promise, to satisfy customers, and to contribute the creativity and innovation required to grow the company.

Organizational gravity has a dual attraction function: it attracts not only talent and customers, but it also attracts positive public opinion and the attention of the investor community.

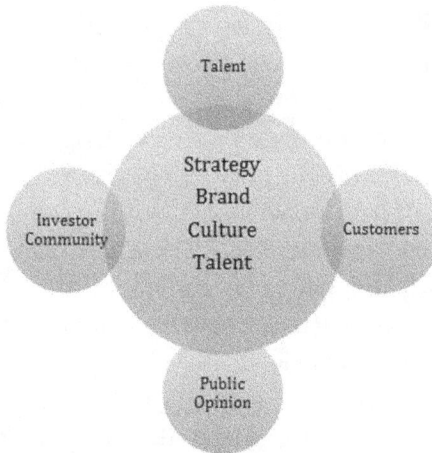

ORGANIZATIONAL GRAVITY

To better understand the idea of organizational mass and how it creates organizational gravity, we use a triangle, which we divide into four distinct quadrants. Each quadrant represents the key elements of organizational gravity:

- Business growth strategy
- Brand
- Culture
- Talent development and management

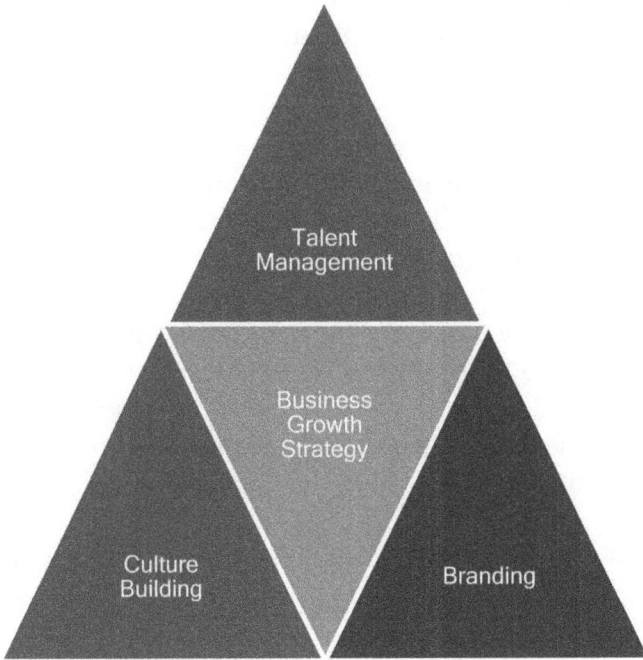

TWO REASONS TO BECOME A GRAVITATIONAL ORGANIZATION

The first reason to become a gravitational organization is talent acquisition—a leading challenge for many organizations.

The Kaufman Foundation conducted a survey with entrepreneurs at the 2011 Inc. 500 5000 Conference[2] and found that the biggest impediments to growth were "finding qualified people" and "managing fast growth," which represented 61 percent of the responses.

The market for talented employees, however, is skewed. Some companies have little trouble finding employees. Human resources or hiring managers choose from a pile of résumés and letters from people eager to get a job—any job. Yet unless you can select, hire, and transition the right talent, the pile of résumés is, in effect, useless. However, other companies that require technical, sales, scientific, and clinical skills have a very different problem. They have more jobs than there are qualified people to fill them. And their ability to select, hire, and transition the right talent is also critically important.

According to another survey conducted in 2011 by the ManpowerGroup[3], 57 percent of employers said that their talent shortage had a negative impact on their key stakeholders. It also impacts their companies' ability to grow.

The survey found the key factors impacting the employer's ability to fill a position:

- Candidate looking for more pay than is offered
- Poor image of business sector/occupation (i.e., branding)
- Poor image of company and/or its culture
- Undesirable geographic destination

In this book we focus on and help business leaders address the second and third points:

- Poor image of business sector/occupation (i.e., branding)
- Poor image of company and/or its culture

What we have found, and research supports, is that pay is not the primary driver for joining a company, staying with a company, or enjoying job satisfaction. Nor can a business easily change its geographic destination. But it can still be an appealing place to work, and with an increase in the virtual workforce, place (i.e., geography) is becoming less of a factor.

The second reason to become a gravitational organization is to attract and retain customers. No business can succeed without customers.

It doesn't matter whether you have a great idea, a breakthrough product or service, or a brilliant founder. You will not succeed—in fact, you *cannot* succeed—if you cannot

- develop and implement a growth strategy;
- develop recognition in the market (brand awareness and brand promise) for your product or service;

- deliver, through your culture and people, on the promise in a way that's credible and consistent with—and ideally, exceeds—the customers' expectations.

BREAK THE OLD PARADIGM

Today, you are presented with a myriad of ideas, options, and opinions by respectable authors on how to improve organizational performance:

- how to hire and retain people
- how to increase market share
- how to grow your business

What we find is that if you are searching for that "magic bullet"—the one thing that will solve all your problems—you will end up with two outcomes: poor results and less money in your bank account.

One company we know wanted to increase its market share. The owner wanted to extend his geographic reach and attract new customers. He told us he had engaged a firm to help him build his social media presence. We asked him the following questions:

- What is your business growth strategy?
- Who are you targeting?
- What message do you want to send?
- What is your expected growth?
- Do you have (or could he get) the necessary resources (talent and money) to support growth?

In other words, what does the bigger picture look like? He didn't have an answer. He just believed that getting on the social media bandwagon and increasing his presence there would result in increased business. If it were only that simple.

Business growth is not based on addressing one component of the business and believing that growth will follow. Sadly, it won't. Growth is much more complicated and holistic than that. The initiative described above was, in effect, a tactic. Tactics, without a corresponding strategy to focus the tactic, are simply a waste of time and money.

There is an old aphorism that's been used in business for decades: If you build a better mousetrap, the world will beat a path to your door. Well, customers will not, unless they know what they are getting (brand), have a reasonable expectation that they in fact will get it in the way they feel was promised (a culture of delivery), and they have a good experience in the process (by and with the talent that's serving them).

For example, Apple doesn't only have a great product. It told the world about its great product; it built a culture that attracted talent and the ability to meet the brand promise; and it continues to be a major force in the marketplace. And this company started in a garage!

You think this is a one-off—rare. Rare, yes; one-off, no. Doable? Absolutely. We want to show you what's possible so you can do it also. Think about Google, PayPal, Zappos, eBay, and Facebook. You may never grow (or want to grow) to the size of these companies, but you sure can grow within your market segment and improve the state of your business like they did.

AN INTEGRATIVE BUSINESS MODEL

Building organizational gravity to support business growth requires an integrative approach:

- a clear strategy that is reflective of the market as it exists and the discipline to implement
- a strong brand presence—so talent will notice you and want to be associated with you and customers will want to buy from you
- a strong culture—so talent will want to join your company and grow with it and customers will enjoy their experience with you

- leadership and talent development—so that once talent becomes part of your organization, they will be nurtured and grow, and customers will benefit from the support and guidance they receive from working with you

In the chapters that follow, we delve into each of the four elements of a gravitational organization:

- business growth strategy
- brand
- culture
- talent development and management

We present each element, its importance, and how it contributes to building a gravitational organization. We also show how the elements intersect to contribute to growth, and talent and customer attraction and retention.

We will also show that addressing any one in isolation will result in an imbalance, creating

- an adverse impact on your ability to attract and retain talent;
- an adverse impact on your ability to attract and retain customers;
- an adverse impact on your ability to grow your business.

Following this chapter, we present the core elements. The follow-up chapter to each core element is a companion chapter. Each companion chapter is a composite of related stand-alone themes and concepts delivered in short segments representing examples, tips, methods, and techniques.

One question we often get from prospects and our clients is, *Where do we start...which element is the most important?* The simple answer is you start from where you are. The more in-depth answer is you need to understand your strengths, your limitations and failures, your resources, and your key opportunities, and you need to develop an executable strategy. Based on our experience, one thing is certain: if you address only part of any one of these elements, there is a very high likelihood that you will not achieve your desired results.

Think of this book as your business gyroscope. Using the metaphor of a rocket launch (which is often how it feels to start and grow a company), there are many components in the rocket that are required to perform well in a coordinated way. If any one were to not perform well, the rocket would start to veer off course and ultimately crash. The purpose of the gyroscope is to keep the rocket on course.

In this book we not only help you build the components so that they perform well for your business, but we also show how they can keep you on a growth trajectory.

PART ONE

◇◇

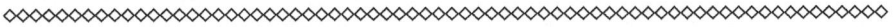

BUSINESS GROWTH STRATEGY

CHAPTER

1

BUSINESS GROWTH STRATEGY

The purpose for making your company a gravitational organization is to grow your business. The reason people go into business is to create a livelihood doing something they are good at and enjoy. The second reason a business exists (or should exist) is to serve its customers and clients better than anyone else in the market. And when a business serves its customers and clients well, there is more demand for its product or service. As demand grows, the business grows.

But rarely does a business grow on its own. Growth doesn't just happen; customers don't just flock to your door to buy from you because you have a trendy product or a cool idea. Businesses grow because they are guided by a *strategy*.

What's your strategy, and how do you identify it and go about implementing it?

Richard Rumelt[1] (*Good Strategy/Bad Strategy, 2011*) describes strategy as developing a cohesive and clear response

1

to the challenge facing your organization. And he goes on to say, "Unlike stand-alone decisions or a goal, 'strategy' is a coherent set of analyses, concepts, policies, arguments, and actions that respond to a high-stakes challenge." It's about making decisions on what to do and what not to do. It's about focus. It's about thoughtful reflection on market opportunities and company capabilities (i.e., attributes, weaknesses, risk potential). It's about a candid assessment of where you are as a company today and where you want to position yourself tomorrow and then defining how you will get there.

The reality is that implementing strategy is not as simple or straightforward as it sounds. Too often you see "blue sky" strategy meetings: endless pontification on all the wonderful products and services the company can provide and how the customers will find its offerings irresistible. But when the strategy session ends and the team shows up for work the next day, the session seems almost like a fun dream—but now it's time to wake up and get back to work. Not following through and implementing the action plans made at the strategy session just does not work.

A good strategy not only helps set direction for the company, but it also helps you acquire and keep talented employees. It helps because employees want to feel part of the whole: to know where the business is headed, what is most important, and how they fit in. Having nonexistent, poor, or competing growth strategies—or even an uncommunicated strategy—is reckless and totally avoidable.

Executives are responsible for developing the growth strategy, sometimes referred to as the strategic direction of the company; the employees fill in the details and create innovative ways to execute the plan; and then the strategy is implemented. It's truly a synergistic relationship. And it's the intersection of the three circles that catapults growth.

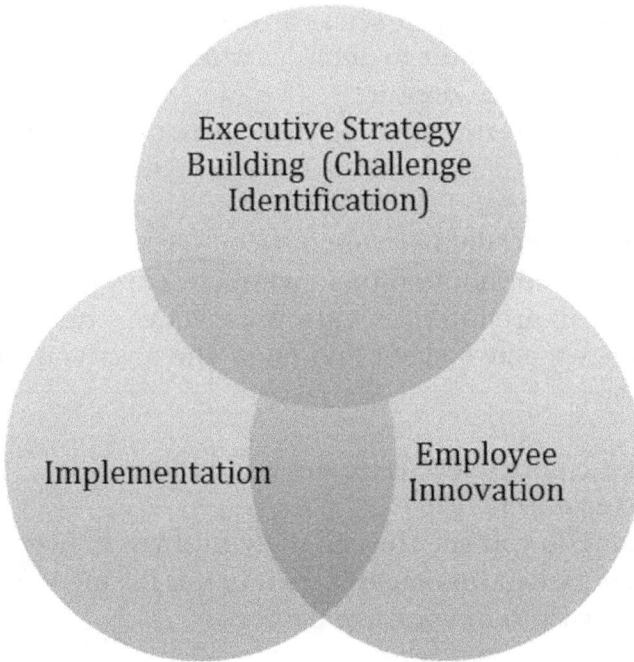

The Strategy Creation Relationship

How Do You Start?

In order to develop your strategy, you must first start with defining or revisiting the Mission, Vision, and Values of your business. While some say, "We don't need to do that," or "There's simply not time," we strongly disagree. A clear and meaningful vision, mission, and set of core values serve as the underpinning—the strategic framework—of who your company is, what you are here to do, and what's most important in the process of your work. And this is one thing employees continually ask for—to understand the big picture—where the organization is headed and what's most important in getting there.

Quick Definitions

Your *Mission* is your statement of purpose: why you exist; what you are here to do.

Your *Vision* is how you see your company in its ideal future state. What do you want to achieve, what value do you want to bring, and what's the dream?

Your *Values* are the guiding principles upon which you will run the company, make decisions, treat your customers, and treat your employees.

So if you haven't defined your Mission, Vision, and Values, you are missing the foundation upon which to grow your business.

Imagine you are interviewing a prospective employee or talking with a prospective client and he or she asks you the following questions:

- What can employees expect in and from this organization?
- Where do you see the company in three to five years?
- What makes this organization better for me to do business with than your competitors?

What would your answers be?

Once the Mission, Vision, and Values have been defined for the organization, there are three basic questions you need to address for strategy building:

5. Where are you now? (an assessment of your current state)
6. Where do you want to be? (your ideal future state)
7. How are you going to get there?

The gap between numbers one and two above represents your challenge, and how you deal with that challenge is represented in number three.

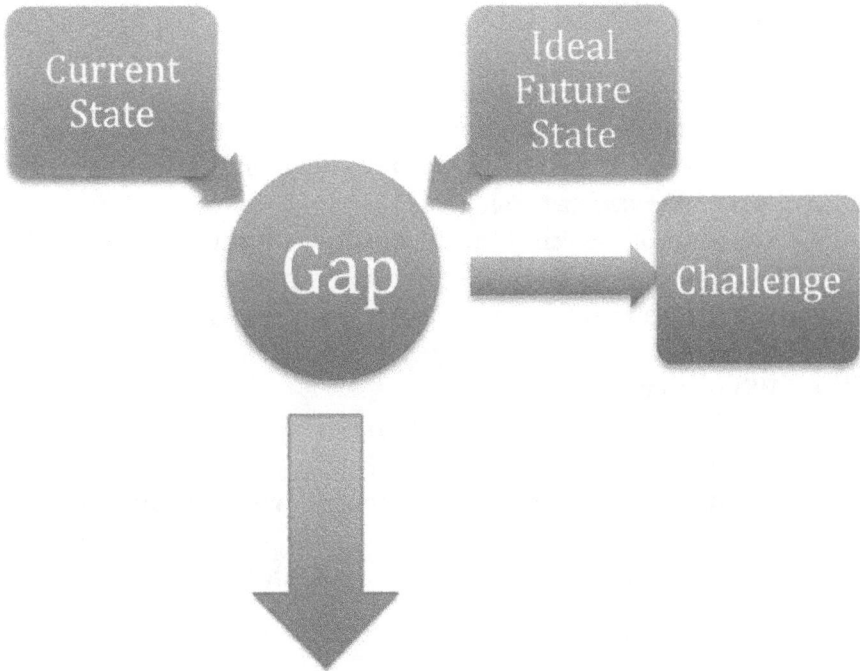

Strategy: The plan to close the gap, prioritized and sequenced

Don't get caught up in the apparent simplicity of these three questions. Answered seriously, they are far from simple questions. To honestly define "where you are now" takes looking deep into the realities of your current business. It takes a clear understanding of what you do and how you do it.

A STRATEGIC PLANNING APPROACH

When we work with our clients on strategic planning, we use a series of exercises to help guide the client's thought process as he or she works to assess vision and sets goals to close the gap.

We start by introducing a series of questions that we feel are important for the business leaders to consider. These questions are top of mind throughout the strategic planning process:

- Who are we?
- What are we here to do?
- What's most important to us?
- What do we want to achieve?
- What's working and how do we know it's working? (*performance indicators*)
- What's not working, and how do we know it's not working? (potential issues/needs to be resolved)
- What else can we do or do we want/need? And how will we know it is working? (*performance indicators*)
- What do we need to avoid?
- What do we need to stop doing?
- What do we need to preserve?
- What else could we do to prepare for worst and best case scenarios?
- What are our next best steps to sustain us now and to best position our growth?

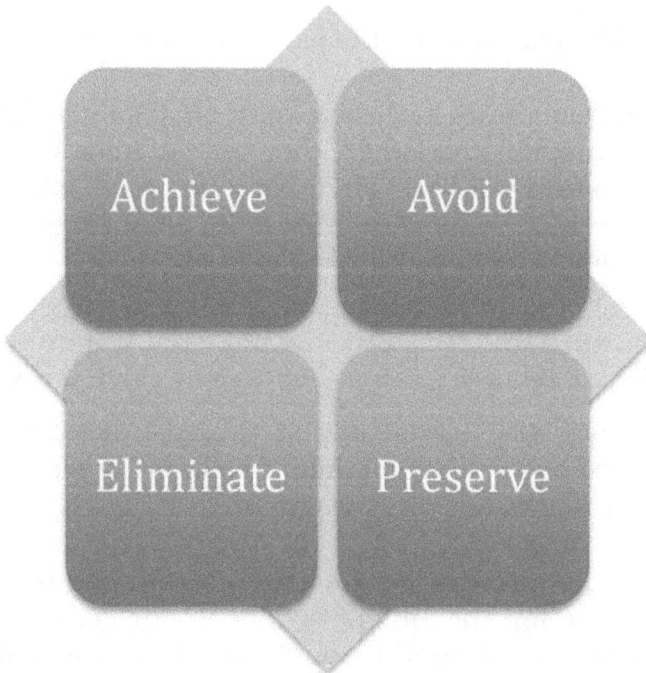

Achieve

Avoid

Eliminate

Preserve

In addition to a traditional SWOT analysis (to identify your strengths, weaknesses, opportunities and threats), you will also want to examine what you want to Achieve, Eliminate, Avoid, and Preserve. This is a variation on the SWOT analysis, and specifically focuses on:

- What you want to Achieve in the next 12 to 36 months
    - o At this point, what you want to achieve, is a brainstorming session and frames the thinking of the group.
- What is important to Eliminate
    - o Oftentimes, executive teams do not spend sufficient time thinking about what should **not** be done.
    - o Eliminating activities can free up resources to support what the executive team wants to achieve
- What actions and initiatives you need to Avoid
    - o This includes activities (or behaviors) that can be detrimental to the organization if pursued. An example would be a "one-off" product or service line because one potential client thought it would be interesting.
- What is important (foundationally important) to the organization and must be Preserved.
    - o A positive culture is an example
    - o A branding approach that resonates with the market
    - o The way new hires are integrated in the company

These four activities are inter-related. For example, growing a business needs resources. An executive team would not be best served if they decided to cut back on the new hire integration initiative to free up resources for a new initiative.

Next is to examine the Trends & Influencers in the marketplace. For example, consider the following elements from both current condition and anticipated changes in terms of how they can impact your business. Generally, this will surface key enablers you will want to optimize and potential business disablers you will need to mitigate for.

- social trends
- competitive landscape of your market
- economic state
- environmental issues
- political landscape
- technological use and advances in your sector
- industry/supplier trends
- customer relationships
- customer satisfaction and expressed needs and interests

Now some of these may be more relevant to your business than others. But sometimes there are influencers that initially may not appear to be that important but truly are. Social trends for example. These happen slowly, but they nevertheless can be relevant to the long-term viability of your business. One of the more obvious ones is the babyboomers who are reaching retirement age and leaving the corporation. On one hand they represent a new market, on the other, as they leave the corporation, will their replacements be as friendly to your business as their predecessor was?

Finally, identify what you need to do to become distinctive and create a competitive edge. Consider what it would take to help you achieve dominance in the market.

A Note on Engaging Employees in the Process

Talented employees want to be part of the business, and one of the best ways to make them part of the business is to involve them in strategy formulation, which can be done simply through soliciting their feedback, thoughts, and observations. At the very least, employees should be given the opportunity to contribute to the execution (action) plan of the strategy—as they are the one's who will be implementing it.

Employees who feel they are part of designing the future have a much higher likelihood of being enthusiastic participants in helping to create that future. In other words, the change required to implement a new strategy is much less of a barrier when the employees are involved from the early stages.

On to the Plan

After thoughtful assessment, we work with the group to create a high-level implementation (action) plan that includes the following criteria:

- What will be done? (the objectives, key tasks and activities)
- When will it be done? (timeline)
- What resources are anticipated? (budget implications)
- Who is responsible for getting it done? (owners)

Remember, unless you are a solopreneur, employees will be executing the plan, so empower them to innovate and add the details of implementation from the high-level plan. Engagement (greater ownership), quality, and efficiency will be a result.

Coaching Note:

As you go through the strategic planning process, make sure to consider how your proposed strategies align directly to your business purpose (or mission) and values. Be willing to eliminate strategies that do not directly lead to your objectives in the near term, that require resources you do not have, or put you at excess risk. Remember that resources (people, time, money, facilities, etc.) are required to implement each strategy, and these must be determined (or at least projected) to ensure consistent results. A major and common error is not predicting and dedicating the necessary resources needed to execute the plan. That's one of the reasons plans do not come to fruition and why strategic planning outcomes are often so dismal.

GROWTH INVOLVES CHOICES

Strategy comes down to choices, and because there are choices, the power to move forward in a focused, strategic direction requires the ability and willingness to make decisions. You can't do everything. You can't placate the participants in the process by giving everyone something they want. This is not politics; it's business. Business is about choices, timely decisions, and the courage to take action to move forward.

CASE EXAMPLES

A small, research-oriented company that had been in business for ten years was modestly successful. The owners (three partners) were concerned, however, that although they were able to come up with a strategic plan every year, they were not disciplined enough to implement the tactics required to achieve the plan. And they really didn't have to. Business came in, and they were comfortable. The issue for them was that they weren't growing. One of the greatest inhibitors to growth we find in small businesses (and in larger ones too, by the way) is success. Success can mask many problems, and because success often results in financial gains, money can temporarily cover up poor strategy.

The owners engaged us to refocus their efforts on growth, and here is a high-level review of what we helped them to do:

- Look deep inside themselves and their business, and discover they were missing a number of ingredients for growth success
- Develop their purpose (or mission) statement
- Establish company values to guide their work and serve their clients
- Create a strategic vision (ideal future state)
- Identify their target market and the market niche
- Identify key strategies and tactics to implement their vision, and create accountability by assigning those to lead individuals (progress on tactics was reviewed quarterly, with general updates given monthly)

- Embed candid discussion into their regular meetings regarding how they worked together and how work should be distributed to take advantage of each partner's strengths
- Develop and implement tracking and reporting tools and a process to monitor sales
- Create a financial reporting system and monthly discipline in review
- Re-brand to update their brand message as they had outgrown their prior one
- Develop an exit strategy and implement early phases of the plan

The business owners started this initiative in 2008. The next year marked the company's best financial performance in its ten-year history. But success didn't stop there—top line revenue in 2010 was almost 40 percent higher than in 2009, without a deterioration in net income. This increase was accomplished during the worst economic downturn since the Great Depression. And revenue continues to improve each year as of this writing.

So what really happened? Were they lucky? Were they in the right place at the right time? No, neither of these can explain their growth. What they did was stop thinking small. They stopped behaving like a "mom and pop shop," and they decided to focus on growth using a targeted and consistent approach.

Another company we worked with was looking to increase sales. Its model was to focus on companies in the manufacturing industry that did not have a focused and organized sales initiative. It provided these companies with a sales system. Growth was initially defined as finding more companies to represent. What the company had to offer was a robust database of potential clients within the different manufacturing sectors.

As the strategy developed, the company we worked with realized that its biggest asset was the information it collected and stored on manufacturers. And the owners further realized that this information would also be beneficial to buyers, who need to source companies to support their manufacturing programs.

The strategy session enabled them to redefine their strength (i.e., their competitive advantage) and at the same time open up a new market opportunity (buyers).

SUMMARY

As a business owner, you will find that there is a plethora of books, articles, and ideas on how to create a strategic plan or conduct a strategic visioning process. We encourage you not to make this more complicated than is necessary. When creating a strategic plan, understand that the most important outcome is an executable plan that has organizational buy-in and with which you are committed to follow through.

There are plans that, no matter how you look at them, are not executable. They are too vague or too complicated, or there is little company buy-in. Some plans are executable, but the discipline to execute them is not present within the company.

Having a strategic plan/vision means you are only 25 percent toward your goal. Having an executable strategic plan means you are 50 percent toward your goal. You can reach your goal only if you execute.

So hold off on the complicated and convoluted, and work toward identifying a direction that makes sense for your company in these times and with the resources you have. One of the most powerful components you can embed into the plan is the innovating thinking that we discussed earlier in this chapter.

Growth is complicated and requires attention. And strategy is a prime directive of the business leaders/owners. Providing leadership by setting direction, communicating a clear strategy, focusing on execution, and then letting your employees contribute their best will grow your business and distinguish it from others. Thinking small will keep you small; thinking big and planning big will lay the path to your growth.

And remember what George Patton said about planning: A good plan, violently executed now, is better than a perfect plan next week.

CHAPTER

2

Business Growth Strategy Supplement: Tips and Techniques to Help with Strategy Formulation and Guidance

Strategic Planning

Is strategic planning worth your time?

"No. Not now," is a common response, particularly in the last several years.

There are many uncertainties as we enter the second decade of the 21st century perhaps more than ever in recent business history, businesses need a strategic direction. A strategic direction does not limit flexibility and assumes opportunistic quick decision-making. Traditional strategic planning, on the other hand, defines and thereby can be construed to prescribe business focus and initiative, thus limiting opportunistic decision-making (at least it has the tendency to do so). Let's expand that definition or past practice a bit to what we call *establishing a strategic framework*—that is, aligning around the values and underlying principles that drive your business and the best ways to move you forward to accomplish your goals.

A strategic direction results in executives choosing a focused direction for the company. For example, Office Depot sells office supplies, including pens and paper. As reported in the *Wall Street Journal*[1] (January 25, 2010), the CEO, Mr. Odland, decided to review the budget monthly. During one of his reviews, managers told him that cash-strapped customers no longer wanted to buy pens or printer paper in bulk packages. So what did the company do? It started selling single pens and smaller quantities of printer paper. The new practice was a success. Trends (customer needs) were observed, and demands were responded to.

Office Depot didn't get out of the office supply business. It just modified how it did its business.

Using a compass analogy, creating a strategic plan is like setting a compass direction to north. A strategic direction is like setting the direction to northwest, with the flexibility to accommodate northeast as well.

But unless the company is nimble and has the ability and willingness to make quick decisions, the difference between a strategic plan and a strategic direction is an academic and useless discussion.

Flexibility can be a cultural shift for some organizations; quick decision-making, however, is a learned skill.

Remember, when making decisions, rely on facts and evidence to the extent possible. Experiential-based decision-making (long on experience and short on facts) is dangerous and reckless behavior. In fact, what we find is more companies beginning to embrace data analytics to support their decision-making. But even though more companies are doing this, the preponderance of companies are not. And there lies the possibility of gaining a competitive advantage through data analytics.

When making decisions, remember to do the following:

- Gather the data.
- Objectively analyze the data, including assessing market trends and influencing factors.
- Identify the issues to be addressed based on the data.
- Evaluate the alternatives for addressing the issues.
  - o Separate the musts from the wants and never sacrifice a must for a want.
- Assess the risks and benefits for each alternative.
- Decide: take action.
- Implement: follow-through in a managed manner—that is, in an accountable (by person and initiative and time-table) fashion to ensure progress and to monitor results.

Setting a strategic direction is valuable, and being flexible and making quick and informed decisions is how businesses will navigate successfully through the economic recovery.

SETTING A DIRECTION AND TAKING ACTION

Oliver Wendell Homes said, "The greatest thing in the world is not so much where we are, but in what direction we are moving."

Direction is first revealed by understanding the marketplace and how it impacts your business. But knowing is not doing, and doing generates business growth! Once you assess the market and find where you are competitively, you need to set a clear direction. As the Cheshire Cat said to Alice in *Alice's Adventures in Wonderland*[2], "If you don't know where you want to get to, it doesn't matter which path you take." But for your business, it matters, and it matters a lot. So identifying the direction you want to move toward is the critical next step.

The standard approach is to create a strategic plan. But we find that creating a strategic plan often turns out to be an exercise only, and shortly thereafter the participants go back to their offices to do their "real jobs" and revert to how they were doing business up until then. And of course this is well known and widely discussed. Yet somehow, some businesses continue to embark on elaborate strategic planning exercises and then have little to no meaningful follow-up. There is a better way.

In setting a strategic direction, we recommend the following eight steps:

1. Conduct a strategic visioning session.
2. Define or validate the company vision statement (ideal future state).
3. Define or validate the company mission (purpose) statement.
4. Identify or validate the company values (what's most important to guide the work and fashion the climate of the organization).
5. Prepare an implementation plan (one that is doable and affordable, considering the resources available) that is actionable, including tasks, measures, and timelines, and those accountable for them.
6. Identify and implement the best leadership and management structure to support the operations to achieve the plan.
7. Evaluate progress quarterly and course-correct when needed.
8. Hold leaders accountable for performance, that is, the results they produce.

These eight steps are simple and straightforward. We strongly recommend avoiding complexity in the process. If the strategic plan is complex, unwieldy, or convoluted—if the vision and mission statements are hard to understand and not easy to remember and articulate; if the value statements do not honestly reflect organizational behavior; if there is nonexistent or ineffective leadership, and no actionable plan and no accountability—success and growth will elude you. As the old saying goes, "Even a stopped watch is right twice a day." In your business, don't be a stopped watch.

DEFINING YOUR STRATEGIC CORE STATEMENTS

In addition to the eight steps defined above, we have three key tips for developing your strategic core statements:

1. Short trumps long. Why? Because the core statements need to be concise enough to read or hear quickly and short enough to remember for repetition. If statements are too long, people can't determine the core spirit of the message. And it's the core spirit of the message that helps them understand you and your brand!
2. Use some emotionally appealing language, as it is more interesting to read and easier to remember. (Remember that while people want facts, they are driven by and make decisions based on their emotions. So why not meet them there to make the facts and emotional language more meaningful?)
3. Simple beats complex. You want easily understandable and repeatable. A message regarding who you are and why you exist (your purpose/mission), your guiding values and organizational drivers (your core values or value statements), and what you are working to create (your vision—the ideal future state) need to be focused. People cannot quickly interpret nor remember complex or elaborate declarations.

Lastly, we give you one of our current favorite examples in vision and vision statements from Zappos[3], a leader in online sales through excellence in customer service. The company leaders achieve excellence through focus on their culture, with the strategic core statements driving their culture through engagement and empowerment of their employees. In 1999, Zappos started in online shoe sales and now is a vibrant and high-growth company that continues to expand its offerings (from shoes to clothing to accessories) and has recently gone international with over three million products available. Its goal is to be the premier online shopping experience.

Zappos Vision Statement:

- One day, 30 percent of all retail transactions in the United States will be online.
- People will buy from the company with the best service and the best selection.
- Zappos.com will be that online store.

Zappos Family Ten Core Values[4:]

- Deliver WOW through service.
- Embrace and drive change.
- Create fun and a little weirdness.
- Be adventurous, creative, and open-minded.
- Pursue growth and learning.
- Build open and honest relationships with communication.
- Build a positive team and family spirit.
- Do more with less.
- Be passionate and determined.
- Be humble.

CREATING A STRATEGIC VISION — ARE YOU MAKING THE THREE MISTAKES MOST ORGANIZATIONS UNKNOWINGLY MAKE?

Have you seen the effects of "success blindness"? Even in this economy, there are still many successful businesses.

Success blindness is a condition in which success can be your greatest impediment to growth and future success. Success hides many ills. It masks fundamental weaknesses in the business and can lead to poor decisions—decisions that could be fatal to your business. We've all heard the expression, "They're just throwing money at the problem." Well, today money is scarce for many. And, simply stated, many businesses can no longer afford to throw money at problems to fix them.

We need a better approach, and it starts with creating a sound strategic vision. While your leadership team works on creating a new strategic vision, be careful to avoid these three mistakes that most organizations unknowingly make.

Three Top Mistakes Business Leaders Make While Creating Their New Strategic Vision and Direction

1. Failing to look at the organization's current strategic vision for relevance and how the market has changed. Before you even start thinking about creating a new vision for your organization, you need to think about these two things:

- Is your past/current strategic vision still relevant in today's economy?
- Has your market changed? For the better or for worse?

If you were selling subprime mortgages your market has changed for the worse. If, on the other hand, you are selling goods or services to Apple, Wal-Mart, or Target, then you are likely doing reasonably well.

Strategy is multidimensional, and what was successful in the past may not be successful in the future. Context and situation require change, or, at the very least, reevaluation and validation. Without a current, sound strategic vision, there is no direction for your company, and forward momentum will become unlikely. Defining a strategic vision is the starting point as business growth resumes.

2. Failing to ask critical questions to assess the health of your business. You see, far too often, small- to medium-sized businesses fail to take an objective and dispassionate view of their operations when planning for their future. In many cases, they focus on only one component of the business, such as sales. How can you determine how to best position your organization for the future? In chapter 1, we presented twelve questions every business owner should ask as part of the strategic-visioning process.

It is critical to ask and listen to your team's responses to these questions when creating your new strategic vision.

And last, *mistake number three*, which is highly interdependent with number two and most critical to execution:

3. Failing to align your leadership team with the new strategic vision of where you are headed. If only you or a few of the executives address the questions above in framing out and defining your strategic direction, a gap results—a lack of knowledge by the very staff who will be making the vision happen (in other words, *executing*). Not being aware of organizational priorities results in disarray due to individual agendas and priorities. (Think of individual employees as arrows pointing in different directions, versus focus and energy pointing in a clear and common direction.)

For example, one of our consulting clients was running a successful research business in the medical industry with a strong client base. The work product was good, as were sales. And for the most part, clients were satisfied. What wasn't working well was the leadership team. Why? Talented researchers were promoted to leadership positions with little (or no) management experience. This created a "learning curve" both for the newly promoted managers (learning how to be a manager) and their employees (learning how to cope with the new manager's learning how to be a manager). The new managers who were thrown into leadership roles brought their baggage with them—the politics, behaviors, and opinions they had as subordinates. No time was spent working to align the new leadership team with the organizational vision and to align the team with itself. As a result, frustration grew—in both the new managers and the employees—and employee turnover became high. In a short time, clients felt the impact.

Lack of a commonly understood strategic direction leads to misaligned efforts and, frankly, to poor decisions—which can be fatal to your business.

The recession has changed many businesses forever. What once were opportune and successful strategies in the past may no longer work. And believing you will soon return to "business as usual" is dangerous thinking.

Through addressing these three mistakes, you can resurface from the recession by taking an intentional, dispassionate look at your current market situation, asking the tough questions, and defining a strategic vision that is desired and doable by you and your staff.

Understanding How the Marketplace Impacts You

One of the most damaging things you can do to your business is to build your strategy based on the generalities you read about in the business and commercial press or you hear about at networking events. So our first recommendation is *get the facts straight.* Before you start concluding what is or is not happening to/for your business in this market—understand what impacts your business.

Five ideas for doing this are listed below:

1. Read about issues impacting your marketplace (positive and negative industry trends) from more than one source. Don't make assumptions from the headline only; look a bit deeper for information that truly impacts your

business or organization and resonates with you on the reality of what is happening in your business.

2. Look for facts that validate your day-to-day reality (and not just opinions).

3. Read about what successful businesses in your market are doing today (specifically strategies and actions taken), and determine how this applies to your business (ideally for replication).

4. Talk with clients and customers about their businesses; ask them what they are interested in, what's working or not working for them, and what has changed for them in the current economy. In other words, learn about their market. It will give you ideas on how to serve them better, and you can accelerate your responsiveness and hone your competitive edge.

5. Be a healthy skeptic, and look at how trends can impact your business, both positively as enablers and negatively as disablers, such as these:
   a. social trends – demographics and psychodemographics
   b. competition – current, those exiting the market, and new entrants
   c. economics – macroeconomic, microeconomic, and behavioral
   d. environmental – the green movement is building momentum
   e. political – new legislation and regulations
   f. technology and social media as key drivers.

The point remains—get and use data to understand your marketplace and how your business is doing in it.

Generalities can be dangerous—avoid reacting to them and take the time to "dig into the details" to make valid and justifiable decisions for your business/organization—then make your decisions.

Implementing Your Strategic Directives: Don't Be One of the Many Failed Plans

You've heard it before: "We've got the strategy set, we know what needs to be done, and now the rest is easy."

We hear it from business owners who are starting a new initiative, who are starting a business, and who are developing a growth initiative. We hear it a lot.

Yet strategy is successfully implemented less than 50 percent of the time. Some believe it is as low as 10 to 30 percent. And even worse, IT projects are infamous for their low implementation success rates.

And one reason, as described by Richard Rumelt[5] in his book *Good Strategy/Bad Strategy: The Difference and Why It Matters*, is that it's not strategy that's being developed but goals. Goals are easy—we want to grow 10 percent next year. The hard part is learning how to grow by 10 percent.

Consider this regarding a 10 percent growth initiative:

- What do you need to do, specifically, to grow?
- And first—is this, in fact, the right thing to do? (You need to be able to answer and agree with the "why" aspect)
    - o Does it address the barriers to growth as they exist for your company at this moment in the marketplace?
    - o Who will do it?
        - □ And what will they have to forego to support the growth target? In other words, what will not get done by them to support the new goal?
        - □ Do you know if you have the resources (cash, time, talent) to do it?
        - □ And what implication does this really have for your company?

Clearly, answering these questions is the harder part.

Is it any wonder then that implementing goals (which is often misnamed "implementing strategy") is so difficult?

Our caution and support to you as a business owner or a leader in a business: it is important not to have your employees suffer through attempting to implement a poorly thought-out goal.

Developing strategy is a challenge. It takes thoughtfulness and time. The goal is the easy part—figuring out the best way forward is much more challenging. As you develop strategy to move toward your goal, you need to address the questions above and to define actions and the consequences of those actions on your business. Your success rate will be much higher if you take the time to do this.

So it's one thing to plan; it's quite another to do something about what you planned.

Strategy formulation—that is, alignment and planning—is the starting point, and implementation (or execution) is where most well-intentioned companies fail.

Once you are clear and aligned in your strategic direction (you have agreed upon your key strategic goals), you must identify what is the best way to get you there. In other words, what's the plan? The plan should take into account what is already working, what is not, and what needs to be done to achieve your strategic goal(s).

In chapter 1 we stressed the importance of *Implementation* in the strategic planning/visioning process. In fact, we believe that successful implementation is the "secret sauce," if you will, in the strategy-setting process. Below, we expand on the initial points made in chapter 1 and offer nine steps for creating an implementation plan:

1. Prioritize the strategic goals to drive focus and align efforts/energies.

2. Create an implementation plan for each of the strategic goals chosen for implementation. Implementation planning worksheets should be completed for each strategic goal, which establish a common document for team awareness and monitoring and can be ultimately used as a frame-up for an annual work plan.
3. Define specific tactics or actions that must be taken to achieve the strategic goal.
4. Assign accountability (i.e., a defined person as the lead who is responsible for ensuring that the plan is implemented).
5. Define success measures (metrics) for each tactic in the implementation plan.
6. Estimate the cost to achieve each specific tactic.
7. Assign a target date for the completion of each tactic.
8. Meet regularly (at least quarterly) to review progress, celebrate success, and determine necessary course-correction (including opportunistic events that may have since emerged).
9. Hold the person responsible accountable.

And add up the costs in time and resources to accomplish the goals you set out to accomplish. Now ask yourself these questions:

1. Do we have the resources to accomplish these goals?
2. What will we need to forgo (if anything) in order to accomplish these goals?

This part is the pragmatic part of the process. And it is much better to know up front about the barriers or realities you are likely to face than when you are well into the implementation process.

Implementation planning is critical to successfully achieving the goals, aspirations, and growth strategies identified and planned for in the strategic process. Failing to implement is like buying a new car and losing the key. It's nice to look at, but it doesn't get you where you want to go.

IS YOUR SUCCESS YOUR BIGGEST PROBLEM?

Are you a business owner whose current success is keeping you from being very successful? Are you a manager who so enjoys your success that it is actually keeping you from growing your division or department? Are you no longer listening, no longer taking risks, and no longer making the hard decisions?

Some owners, leaders, and managers talk about competition but fail to do anything about it. Content with success, they slowly become risk-averse and complacent. Good is good enough; don't rock the boat; why mess with a good thing? We behave like the frog dropped into a pot of cold water. As the pot heats, the frog continues to swim around until the water boils and the frog is done. Change happened so slowly, the frog never saw it coming.

There was a mid-sized consulting company (approximately five hundred employees) in the Midwest. It successfully completed an IPO (initial public offering, which was very popular in the mid-nineties). It was a very successful company—one of the top two firms in its market. At one point, its market value approached a half billion dollars.

What did they do with the money?

- They bought other companies—but did not have an integration strategy.
- They leased more office space.
- They increased the number of executives (overhead).

At one point, the company had close to fifteen hundred employees, who were working in silos—sometimes at cross-purposes—and spending money. When the pullback in technology started in 2000, the company was poorly positioned to compete. But pleased with their success, they continued doing more of the same, without looking forward and taking action based on what was on the horizon. The company was eventually sold.

How do you know if success is keeping you from being successful? Consider the following questions:

- Is your revenue growing?
- Is it growing faster or slower than your competition's? (Do you know?)
- Is your customer base growing?
- Is there a product or service being introduced (or anticipated) that could make your product or service obsolete?
- Are your departments or staff working with, against, or without the support of one another?
- Are your best employees leaving?
- Are you able to attract top talent?
- Are you introducing new products or services into the marketplace and adjusting your offerings with the trends and forecasts?

You may think that these points are nonsense. How can a company grow in this economy? But that's complacency thinking. Companies are growing in this economy; businesses are maintaining market share. It's your choice. As Marshall Goldsmith so powerfully titled one of his most popular and widely read books, *What Got You Here, Won't Get You There.*

COMPLACENCY IN STRATEGY CAN RUIN YOUR BUSINESS

Strategy is a word that is often bandied about in business circles. It can get pretty expansive: strategic planning, marketing strategy, financial strategy, product strategy, a strategy for developing a strategy—and it's used as if everyone clearly understands what it means.

Let's start with what strategy is not. It is not a goal; it is not an objective; it's not an exercise. It is an approach—the means to your end, which

- identifies an unmet need in the market—an opportunity to be in a place or do things where the competitors are not;

- aligns your ability to address that need, resulting in a competitive advantage for your company;
- considers the barriers that can interfere with execution;
- assesses what your company needs to do to execute the strategy;
- identifies the resources to do it.

We've recently seen two large, high-visibility companies stumble: Research In Motion (the maker of Blackberry) and Borders. Borders paid the ultimate price for a poor strategy—the company filed for bankruptcy on February 16, 2011.

RIM suffered a dramatic drop in market share. As we wrote earlier, RIM is in third place behind smartphones run by Google's Android and the iPhone.

There are many other companies that have failed because of poor strategy and poor execution. (A great strategy is useless in a business sense unless it can be executed.) Look at Wal-Mart and Kmart[6]. Wal-Mart knows how it wants to provide value to its customers and provides it. K-Mart has failed to find and implement a value-driven differentiation strategy.

Small businesses are not immune to the perils of poor strategy; unfortunately, they fail faster due, in part, to poor capitalization. The exciting part, however, is that companies with a good strategy and the ability to execute it can succeed and grow (sometimes spectacularly). Remember, Wal-Mart was once a small five-and-dime (Walton's 5 & 10) in Bentonville, Arkansas.

A question we often get from business owners, however, is, "How can we possibly plan in an unstable economic environment?"

It's a fair question, considering the following:

- Congress and the White House are in an ideological deadlock on how to best address the economic problems we face.
- There is a mismatch in some businesses between the talent they need to grow their businesses and the skills available in the marketplace.

As we have advised in the past, and we advise again—while the economic outlook is unsettling, it is important to understand how your company is doing and how your clients/customers are doing. Some businesses are still doing quite well, even in these tumultuous times.

The *Wall Street Journal* ran an article on an Indiana machine shop business—Bremen Casting Inc. (August 10, 2011)[7]. The company is deciding whether to continue the expansion of its melting metals capacity. The executive team met to decide whether to request an additional $5 million bank loan to complete the expansion. They looked at their customer base (fifteen companies represented 50 percent of sales). They looked at the ordering pattern and concluded that their customer base was solid, and they did not forecast, based on data, a drop in demand. They went forward with the loan and continued to add capacity.

This is a good example of looking at your market as it exists for you and your clients/customers today, rather than extrapolating bad news to your market. One is analytical and proactive; the other is emotional and reactive. Focus on what's real for your business; identify and then focus on the opportunities your competitors will open up for you, based on their overreaction, and act accordingly. It may be just the time for you to become aggressive.

An Absence of Business Common Sense

Too many business leaders, instead of thinking through strategy, are searching for the holy grail of business solutions—the fad that will work, the business trend of the year. And they're willing to spend big money to find it. Yet few do.

In our work with clients, we start by looking at how well they do the basics: responsiveness, relationship-building, and identifying and serving the customers' real needs—the basics that many business leaders seem to take for granted and often overlook.

We sometimes hear when we talk about the basics, "Tell me something I don't know." What many of these businesses don't know is how to successfully accomplish the basics. Knowing isn't synonymous with doing.

We believe that business solutions exist on a continuum. On the far left, we have the low-cost/low-risk options; on the far right, we have the high-cost/high-risk options.

In our opinion—and in our experience—too many business leaders choose to enter into the high-cost/high-risk range of the continuum, thinking bigger or more complex is better and will address everything. Please hear this: It is almost impossible to identify and implement a high-cost/high-risk solution if the business basics are not addressed. (Read: you will likely be wasting your time, money, and resources.)

A case in point is a technology company client who was looking to increase sales of its software products. The company sold nine individual products. We conducted a series of targeted interviews with IT consultants, small business owners, CIOs, and potential customers, and the feedback was consistent. The interviewees felt that the company had an impressive software solution (i.e., good technology), but they could not clearly understand what the company sold, who the buyer was, and what the value proposition was—that is, a concise statement of the improved condition the client will realize (or can expect) as a result of purchasing the product.

We worked with the company to define its market (in this case, the health care market), what it sold, its target customer, and its value proposition.

As a result, the company now concentrates on two key product categories (risk management and quality management), and the team knows and can articulate its target buyers and has a clearly defined value proposition. All of these activities were on the low-cost/low-risk side of the continuum.

Starting with and addressing the low-cost/low-risk options for improvement or growth just makes good business sense, especially if you are a start-up or are in the early stages of business.

THE BUSINESS BASICS: YOU CAN'T SUCCEED WITHOUT THEM

A sports team cannot be successful; a house, car, or structure of any kind cannot be built without addressing and mastering the basics. Why, then, do we believe that we do not have to attend to the basics in business? Businesses fail every year, and some don't fail because the market is bad, or because they had a poor product or service; they fail—or implode—because they did not attend to the basics of building the business.

Imagine a football team taking the field without knowing how to block and tackle. Oh, they can run (or try to run) sophisticated and complex plays, but without the ability to block—the plays fail. On defense, players have a great defensive strategy, but they can't tackle. It only works when teams can block and tackle.

We often hear the phrase in business, "We've got to get back to the basics—blocking and tackling." Yet far too many fail to do so. They talk about it, especially on Monday mornings after the Sunday football games, but talk and action are not the same thing.

Here's our advice on business basics:

1. Develop a product or service that the market needs and will buy;
2. Create a strategic vision for the business;
3. Clearly define value statements;
4. Have a brand that defines your promise to the market;
5. Provide an organizational structure that will allow the business to execute effectively;
6. Hire executives and managers who are not only good content experts, but also good managers (they are different and they are both needed);
7. Create a support infrastructure that can support the business as it is today and that can adjust and grow as the business grows;
8. Use metrics that will enable the executives to monitor progress and identify areas needing improvement;

9. Provide outstanding customer service;
10. Have a succession plan.

We do not pretend to give you the impression that attending to the basics is easy. As a martial artist, I can attest that it is easy to learn how to block, kick, and punch the open space in front of you. It's a much different experience when there is a live body returning the kicks and punches (read: competition).

In business it is essential to learn, develop, and practice the basics—and to improve a little each day. The improvements accumulate, and the business gets stronger and more effective. Then, if you want, you can look at some of the fads—but our guess is you won't need to.

EVIDENCE-BASED BUSINESS GROWTH

Every business owner we meet asks basically the same question: "How do I get my business to grow?" And this question is especially prudent in the post-Great Recession economy.

While the question is admittedly complex, there are ways to reduce the complexity and reduce the mistakes owners make when growing their businesses. The way to do it is to understand, accept, and embrace evidence-based management. Perhaps the best proponent of evidence-based management is Jeffrey Pfeffer (professor of organizational behavior, Stanford Graduate School of Business).

As an example, we know (or should know) that when starting a business, it's important to

1. have a well-defined product or service that meets an unmet need in the marketplace (differentiation strategy);
2. have adequate funding (working capital) to support the business (and yourself) until revenue generated can support the business;
3. have a business development strategy to find, qualify, and sell to customers;

4. have the ability to deliver on your promise (also known as fulfillment, which we see closely tied to your culture).

These are the basics. If you adhere to these four actions, you are very likely to experience early success.

Doing one, two, or three of these well, however, will not make a successful business. Mediocre, maybe, though not viable and sustainable. Why do we say this? Evidence. Evidence that is based on research and personal experience garnered from our work over the years.

Realistically, as a result of our experience in working with businesses, we see far too few actually concentrate on ensuring each of these four areas is addressed. You may wonder why businesses fail to address each of these concerns, considering that the evidence on successful business start-ups is clear. The answer is embarrassingly simple: some people starting new businesses are unaware of the evidence, or they are aware of it but feel their situation is different. Well, we have unfortunate news for those people—their businesses will fail. It's like when a hurricane hits—if you are unprepared, bad things are likely to happen to you and/or your property. The hurricane doesn't care who you are or how confident you are that you will escape harm. Hurricanes do what they do.

Markets are much the same. Your market doesn't care who you are or how confident you are of success. If you're unprepared, harm will come to your business.

Whether you are just starting your business or have recently started it and want to be sure it's on the right track toward growth, we suggest you take these four steps:

1. Conduct an in-depth strategic vision/planning session.
2. Focus on a few actions initially, and do them well.
3. Look at the evidence—keep an open mind.
4. Implement—do what you say you are going to do. Take action, monitor, and course-correct according to evidence.

When starting or growing a business, you must differentiate yourself, and the best way to initially differentiate yourself is by using evidence-based management to start strong.

To learn more about evidence-based management, we suggest you read Jeffrey Pfeffer and Robert I. Sutton's book, *Hard Facts, Dangerous Half-Truths, and Total Nonsense* (Harvard Business School Press, 2006)[8].

BEWARE THE BUSINESS INFLECTION POINT

If you are in business and you are growing, you will hit inflection points. So the question is not *if* they will happen; it's how you will deal with them when they *do* happen.

Andrew Grove describes inflection points in his book *Only the Paranoid Survive*[9]. An inflection point occurs when the old strategic order dissolves and gives way to the new, allowing the business to ascend to new heights. However, if you don't navigate your way through an inflection point, you go through a peak, and after the peak, business declines. It's around the inflection points that managers puzzle and observe, "Things are different. Something has changed."

For many, the following will be a familiar scenario. You start your business, you get some customers, probably in the "family and friends" category, provide good service, and you start to grow. As you grow, you find yourself with less and less time to find new customers, serve current customers, and retain customers. You are likely not to have a growth plan and not much of a support structure for your business. A moment of truth has arrived—you have just hit an inflection point. And how you deal with it will determine whether your business continues to grow, or whether it begins a slow and painful decline.

The euphoria of early business success is inescapable, but it can also be a mental fog machine. Early success blinds you to the realities of building your business. We have heard business owners say, "We don't need to brand ourselves; we've done okay so far without it." Or "My accountant takes care of my books; why do I need financial statements? That's a waste of time and money." Or we see the tendency of business owners to chase after every new market segment without realizing each one represents a different approach and may require different resources. You may have heard these stories; you may have experienced them yourself.

Identifying and managing through an inflection point is important for the health and welfare of your business. And if you are new to business or new to running a company, do realize that inflection points exist, and they are to be taken very seriously. To loosely paraphrase Marshall Goldsmith, what got your business to where it is now will not get you to the next level of business success.

Let's review the common reasons why businesses fail (the list below is adapted from an article by Jay Goltz[10] on NYTimes. com:

- not enough demand for the product or service
- poor management: inexperience, hubris
- growing too fast
- poor financial controls
- lack of capital
- operational inefficiencies
- dysfunctional management team
- lack of a succession plan
- a changing/declining market

If you do not have a sellable product or service or if you do not have adequate capital or if you are in a changing/declining market, you simply will not have a viable business.

The tragedy comes when you do have a sellable product or service, when you do have adequate capital, and when you are in a growing market—yet still fail. In this situation recognizing and managing through the inflection points are critical for your business.

When you reach an inflection point, unattended issues such as poor management, poor financial controls, operational inefficiencies, dysfunctional teams, and no succession plan become disproportionately large factors that contribute to business failure. Just as you cannot build a multistory house without a solid foundation, you cannot build a successful business without a foundation of business basics in place.

Business owners can easily get seduced into complacency in a growing market. The aphorism "a rising tide lifts all boats" is accurate. But when the rising tide is seen as operational brilliance in the mind of the business owner, it closes off all ability to receive input and heed warning signs.

In any economy, businesses can be in a "rising tide lifts all boats" phase; others struggle to stay in business. It's becoming more of a challenge to navigate these changing waters of business growth, and good management is required.

If you haven't yet done so, do so now: assess where you are in your business—what's working (and why) and what's not working (and why). Be brutally honest with yourself. Are you reaching an inflection point? If so, what are you doing about it?

GETTING BEYOND THE "PAIN POINT"

On May 6, 1954, Roger Bannister did what many believed was impossible. He broke the four-minute mile.

How does this relate to starting and building a business? Part of the answer is in one of his quotations: "A man who can drive himself further once the effort gets painful is the man who will win." Paraphrased: the business owner who can drive further when it's most difficult (even painful) is the business owner who will succeed.

We see far too many new business owners start with unbridled excitement and enthusiasm. You have a sure-fire winner in your business idea. You can't lose; people will want to buy from you, do business with you. "Why not?" you ask. "We have a great product/service."

Then reality hits. You need to market; you need to get past what at times seems to be a tsunami of no's; you need to work what seem to be ridiculous hours (and, to quote Dr. Seuss[11], initially "for that piffulous pay of two Dooklas a day"); you need to overcome the doubters who watch from the wings and revel in "I told you so." No, it's not easy to start and run a successful business, especially if you lack the conviction and courage that ultimately drive success.

Building a business on your own is challenging. As you hit what we call the "pain points" (inflection points), you are essentially on your own to work through the challenges, overcome the doubts, and manage the risks. (This is one of the reasons we recommend partnering when forming a business.)

Successful business owners are like elite athletes. They train; they set goals; they practice through consistent demonstration; and they seek assistance and support (coaching) to help them improve and achieve their goals. They have learned to work beyond the pain.

While these pain points are uncomfortable and trying, they are not only essential to overcome, but they are also ripe with opportunity for learning and growth. And that is our first tip:

- Reframe your thinking about your situation when you find yourself there—metaphorically turn the lights on to forward thinking and action versus allowing yourself to "turn off"—in other words, avoid or resist. And remember, pain points represent business-growth inflection points!
- Identify clearly the issue (the pain point). What is the root cause of the problem?
- Develop options for a solution. It may be simple, or it could be complex based on the issue/root cause. We encourage you to ask for help from a trusted friend, advisor, or mentor, as multiple perspectives will surely help to balance the emotion-laden situation for you. The

situation you face may not be one you have experience dealing with, and a lack of knowledge tends to lead to avoidance.

- Vet the costs/benefits (or pros and cons) of each option, then select the best option to achieve the results you need or desire. Again, another perspective can add a world of value. A good accountability partner will work wonders in helping you accomplish daunting tasks, undesirable tasks, or tasks you have little or no experience dealing with.

- Breakdown the key "next steps" (tasks), and assign them to a timeline (schedule) to ensure you are working toward the solution/improvement. (This step could include farming out tasks or outsourcing to others at this point.)

- Monitor as needed and, when complete, reflect on your learning and the gains from your efforts, and either course-correct using the same tips above; or celebrate your success and thank those who helped you along the way.

We all face pain points as our businesses evolve. What matters is not that they occur, but how we deal with them for the betterment of our business and our customers/clients.

Growing an Imperfect Business: Go for Success, not Perfection

We all have at least one common goal: to grow our businesses. But there is an important question to ask yourself: Is your quest to run a perfect business, or is your intent to run a successful business? While it may be a great intention to run the perfect business, you run the risk of nonstop planning, employee frustration, deteriorating morale, and missed opportunities.

There are leadership traits, which, if left unrecognized, will prevent you from not only recognizing opportunities, but also from reacting fast enough to benefit you, your employees, your customers, and your business. And speed to market is a differentiator, especially for a small business. Perfectionistic traits, which lead to low morale, include the following:

- Failure to delegate—withholding key assignments from your direct reports, because you believe they cannot do the work as well as you can do it.
  - o This also results in them working on meaningless or minor assignments.
- Micromanaging employees' work. This trait is similar to the one above, except that you actually assign and delegate work, but thereafter you tend to tell them what to do and how to do it. You do not allow them to figure out the best means to the end.
- More concern with how the report looks than what it says (being appearance-oriented versus content-oriented)
  - o How many times do you focus on correcting punctuation and grammar when you get a report, or change slide backgrounds and fonts, but provide little or no meaningful feedback on the content?
- Detail (versus strategy) focused—asking for more information when it becomes clear that no one can answer all the questions.
- Everything is important—that is, perfectionistic managers have a hard time determining priorities, and often not much gets done, or gets done well, because the employees are spinning.

And the likely results from this quest for perfection in business are

- delays in making important decisions;
- competition getting to the market before you do;
- you become surprised by events that should have been predictable.

- not capitalizing on the strength of your group and the power of a contributory team;
- people may leave, seeking more challenging work and a more empowering boss.

Perfection is rarely achieved, and we believe it is a fool's goal. Give up the quest for perfection. Good is good enough. As noted above, George S. Patton said, "A good plan violently executed now is better than a perfect plan executed next week." Besides, the market doesn't stand still. Things change, and it is your responsibility to adapt. Don't waste time creating the perfect plan and the perfect business. Develop a good plan; execute it with passion; monitor and make mid-course corrections along the way; work as a real team; and you can celebrate growth and success. And who knows, you may be happily telling someone how you grew and succeeded with an imperfect business.

ALIGNING YOUR EXECUTIVE TEAM

Imagine an executive team in which each executive has his or her own agenda, vision for the company, exit strategy for the business (or for him or her personally), and strategic priorities for the coming year. How successful do you believe this company would be? If you said "unsuccessful," you would be right.

Often, we see companies that fit this profile. An unaligned executive team will not succeed in the marketplace. Members of the team are more vulnerable to competitive pressures than their aligned competitors, and they are prone to higher employee turnover and a dissatisfied and disgruntled workforce, which translates into poor customer service.

Now you may be asking, if an unaligned executive team has such adverse consequences, why would they not become aligned? It seems so obvious. The answer is that they don't know any better. Team alignment is the responsibility of the CEO. What you permit, you promote; and if you permit executives to, in effect, "do their own thing," you will promote and actually encourage this behavior.

In his book *The Founder's Dilemma: Anticipating and Avoiding the Pitfalls That Can Sink a Startup,* Noam Wasserman[12] reports that in a survey of venture capitalists, 65 percent of the failure in their portfolio companies was due to problems with the management team.

Some of the reasons CEOs will permit executives to be unaligned are as follows:

- They believe they are successful enough.
- They are afraid to confront their executives for fear of losing them or retaliation.
- They truly don't believe or are simply unaware there is a problem, at least at the executive level.

Unless the executive team is aligned, meaningful change is not possible. And like the boiling frog story told earlier in the book, when the CEO finally realizes that something needs to change (because employees are leaving; it's difficult to hire good replacements; customers are defecting; the business is starting to fail)—it may be too late.

THE KNOWING–DOING GAP: A COMPETITIVE EDGE

Information has become a commodity. It's easy to access, and there is far more of it than we can digest. We can generalize and say that today most businesses have about (or can access) the same amount of information. If you believe this (and based on our experience, we do), then why don't all businesses perform equally as well? The answer we've found is that they don't do very much with the information they have—they fail to execute.

The "knowing–doing gap" (a concept first presented in a book by Pfeffer and Sutton[13] called *The Knowing–Doing Gap*) isn't created by the lack of information; it's created by the inability to use that information in a way that materially helps your business.

And the knowing-doing gap is endemic in organizations. It is supported and perpetuated by the "the experts," whether they are executives, managers, or consultants. They are the people with the information; they are the people who know how things should be done; they are the people who have the answers. They are also the people who, after the retreat or after the meeting, go back to their offices and assume the heavy lifting has been done. It's now someone else's job. The plan, after all, has been made; the strategy set. Now for the easy part—implementation.

Successful organizations, growing organizations, and market leaders are simply better at *doing*.

If you want to differentiate your business or yourself, if you want to find a competitive edge—you need to execute well, swiftly and consistently. And it doesn't matter if you are a solo practitioner, a small business, or an international conglomerate—execution is the key to business success.

While information is great, results trump information.

PART TWO

BRANDING

PART TWO

CHAPTER

3

BRANDING

What is branding, and why is it important? Simply put, branding is the external message and promise you make to the marketplace (to your present and future customers) about your product or service. Your promise should be different from your competitors. In fact, it *must* be different from your competitors, or you are selling nothing more than an undifferentiated commodity. (And if that's the case, be prepared to drop your price continually.) Branding "gets the word out" about who you are, what you do, and what you stand for, and it positions you as the right company to do business with.

BRANDING, MARKET, BUYER

Think about the brands of companies you know. As you look at this list, see how long it takes for you to clearly recognize and form an opinion about each company's position in the marketplace:

- Nordstrom
- Apple
- Wal-Mart
- Target
- Amazon
- Google
- Zappos
- Yahoo!
- Southwest Airlines
- HP
- US Airways

Each has a recognizable brand. Some are high-end, high-quality, high-service, and high-cost providers. Others are low-service, low-cost providers. Some provide impressive service; others cause premature baldness because you end up pulling your hair out almost every time you have to deal with them. Whether you like them or not is less important than the fact you recognized them. You may even choose to do business with them because of the impression they make on you or choose not to do business with them because of their reputation (i.e., negative brand image).

What's one of the most important commitments someone can make to you? It is a promise. It's powerful. A promise means someone understands what is important to you and understands that one of the best things he or she can do for you is keep his or her promise. Good brands do that.

Weak brands, on the other hand, make promises that they do not keep. How long do you tolerate a person who makes a promise and then breaks it? You may give him or her one more chance (perhaps two) because you believe deep down there is some good there. But when the promises continue to be broken, what do you do? You move on.

We have seen the impact of brand deterioration[1] at HP and Research In Motion (RIM). Bank of America[2] flirted with it a while back when it tried to introduce a five dollar per month fee to use a debit card. It was a bad branding and public relations move, which they had the good sense to retract. Yet, it continues to negatively impact their brand perception.

Netflix[3] stumbled with its botched attempt to introduce a new brand (Qwikster) and when it raised the prices of its combined streaming and DVD plan by 60 percent.

RIM (creator of the Blackberry) could very well be the poster child for grabbing defeat out of the jaws of victory. The company had a dominant position in the smartphone marketplace, only to see it squandered by its inability to meet the brand challenge (supported by a strong technical product) presented by Apple and the various devices that run Google's Android software. Once, the Blackberry commanded a significant share of the market for US mobile subscribers. At the end of June 2012, its reported market share was below 2 percent, well behind Apple's iPhone and Android devices[4]. In fact, one pundit predicted that Blackberry will no longer exist in 2013[5].

Contrast this example with companies building their brands, such as Amazon, Apple, Google, Zappos, and Zynga. These companies, at least as far as we can tell, are working to build and maintain their brands in the marketplace. They are customer attractors. At the same time, their well-aligned recruitment strategies help them build a competitive position in the job market by attracting top talent.

BRAND AND TALENT

While branding is a powerful tool to generate market awareness in current and future customers, it also has another impact: talent acquisition.

As a business leader who wants to grow your organization, you want to attract the most talented people who will best position your company to deliver its promise to the marketplace. Talent, simply stated, makes things happen in an organization. And if you are a service organization, all you have, really, is talent. That is your only significant asset. Take talent out, and what's left? An empty building, some desks, chairs, and computers. And you can be certain—no one grows a company with a building, desks, chairs, and computers.

When we start to think about attracting talent, what's a likely motivation for prospective employees? They want to be associated with something great, something that others also identify as great. It's part of human nature. Great talent is no exception. That's why talented engineers want to work for companies like Google. Professor and author John Sullivan says that Google has created a "recruiting machine"[6] through branding and culture. Google demonstrates the way recruiting is done.

WHAT ARE YOU DOING ABOUT YOUR BRAND?

So, what are you doing about your brand, your expressed promise? What are you doing to be different in the marketplace so that not only great talent notices you, but current and future customers notice you as well?

You don't have to be a Google, an Apple, or some other billion-dollar company. What you have to be is different and remarkable within your niche. You have to be the voice above the voices. How you choose to represent yourself to your market will either encourage or discourage candidates and customers. Consider these four key questions:

What's Your Message to Current and Future Customers? *

What's Your Promise?

Brand

How Is It Different From Your Competitors?

Why Does It Matter to Your Customers

* We refer to customer in this example as composed of the buyers of your products and services and as the talent you want to draw to your company. In truth you are also selling them on the value and benefits of working for you. So at this stage they are an external prospect who you want to convert to an internal employee.

GETTING THE MESSAGE OUT

How you get your message out is important. While we will not address the nuances and complexities of building and maintaining your brand, we do want to mention briefly, especially for the entrepreneur and small business start-up, the importance of early brand *consistency* in these areas:

- logo
- website concept and content
- tagline
- advertisements
- marketing collateral
- social media
- all forms of internal and external expression/communication about the company.

This consistency should carry over to all interactions with prospective employees and current and future customers. Regardless of how your talent enters the recruiting process or how customers and future customers enter your sales cycle, they should see, feel, and interpret who you are, what you stand for, and what they can expect from you based on your brand message.

Yes, a small company just starting out can catch the attention of not only the market, but also the people you want to attract.

How you approach branding and brand consistency is important because the way your message gets out has changed. In the past, common ways to get your message out included traditional outlets:

- print ads in places like newspapers and magazines
- billboards
- radio
- television
- sales staff

It cost a great deal of money to get your message out, and that was a barrier to competitive entry for some start-ups.

Today, it's different. Company size and financial resources are less important in the ability to build a brand. One reason is the communication channel has changed, and the cost to enter and remain in that channel has dropped exponentially.

Today, small businesses, medium-size businesses, and start-up businesses can leverage

- Google ads (or other search engine-based advertising opportunities);
- Google Places;
- social media (e.g., Facebook, LinkedIn, Twitter, and YouTube);
- company websites.

And remember, branding through social media attracts the attention of not only current and future customers; it also attracts the attention of future recruits.

BRAND-NAME JOB ADVERTISING

Companies with strong positive brand recognition can leverage that brand recognition into what is referred to as *strong brand-name job advertising*—the stronger the market brand, the stronger the brand-name job advertising potential.

Interestingly, strong brand-name job advertising is focused more on the internal qualities of the company and its work environment; that is, its culture (which we will address in chapter 3). But you have to know about the company first, and that's where brand comes in. The website HR Management Guide[7] reports that having a competitive position in recruiting is about

- building the impression of the unique approach to employees;
- strong corporate values;
- value of employees as human beings;
- quick decision-making;

- innovative solutions for employees to increase performance and productivity;
- success celebration.

BRAND PERCEPTION AWARENESS

It is essential to know how your brand is perceived by prospective talent and your customers. We find some company owners and executives saying things like, "We really have no competition," "Our quality is the best," "We have the best people," and "We are second to none." Well, we have two simple questions:

1. How do you know?
2. Who says so—you or the customer?

If it's you and your employees saying it, it very well can be delusional; if it's your customers saying it, it's informative. And if your customers are saying it, future talent will notice.

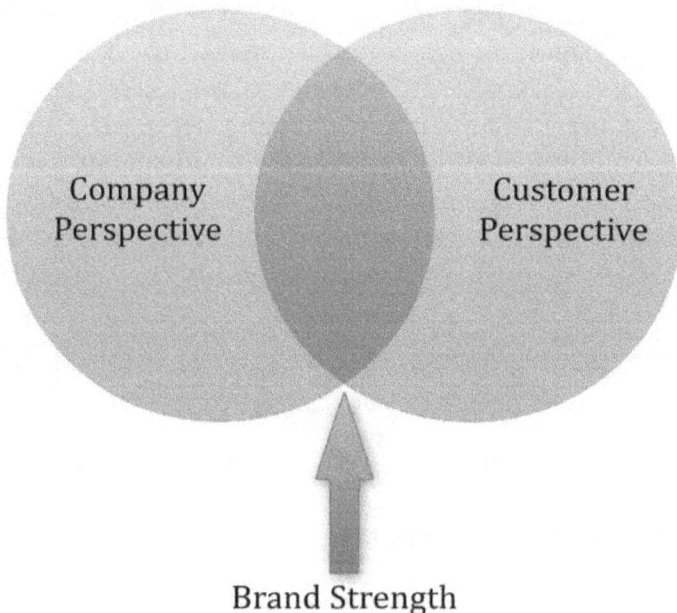

Company Perspective   Customer Perspective

Brand Strength

KNOW HOW THE MARKET PERCEIVES YOU

High-potential future talent (and customers) will learn about you based on what the marketplace says about you. So you better know what it's really saying. The best way to do this is to make a practice of staying close to your customers and periodically asking them, both in survey form and through direct contact, their impression of your company and its products/services.

Customer surveys are a powerful way to understand how your business is perceived by your customers. And it is done by asking your customers how they feel, about you, how well you satisfy their needs, and their likelihood of recommending you/ your company.

Without asking them, you can only guess. And strategy based on guesses is very expensive!

Developing a brand and a branding message drives the consistency you need for the market to recognize you and then work with you. It creates the promise. So then you are done—right? Just create that promise, and your recruiting and customer acquisition challenges will be solved, right?

Well, no. In fact, if you stop here, we can say with certainty that your chance for long-term success and competitive dominance is slim. Unless you consistently and exceptionally deliver that promise, you have set your business up for a fall.

Contrary to current fear-based economics and projections, there are more jobs available in select areas than there are qualified people to fill them. So to grow, you need to fill them; and you will do that only if you are a place people stand in line to join, and that starts with your brand!

And there are customers for unique and compelling products and services. It's a challenge to compete for customers when you are swimming in a sea of sameness, but intelligent, focused, and targeted branding can set you apart, and you will get noticed— by both customers and talent alike

4

BRANDING SUPPLEMENT: A SERIES OF TIPS AND TECHNIQUES TO DRIVE BRAND BUILDING

IS BRANDING REALLY WORTH IT?

The short answer is yes. But if you're not sure and sincerely wonder what a strong brand has to do with getting more business, then read on. Branding is a key strategy to differentiate your business and connect you with your buyer. It is much more than a logo, a tagline, a business card, or a nice website; it is a positioning and differentiation strategy. It is your promise to your buyer and a means to raise your visibility and credibility in the marketplace. It's what makes you stand out in the crowd.

What we commonly hear when we ask companies why clients and customers should do business with them is a list like this one:

- We have the best people.
- We have the best products.
- We have the highest quality.
- We are the premier provider (of the product or service we sell).
- We're different.

Honestly, now, who doesn't say this? No company is going to say it has average people or marginal quality. And what does any of this mean to your buyer? When "everybody" is saying this, then it is no longer being heard and recognized as different enough to catch the buyer's attention.

While branding is a way to represent to the market who you are as a company or organization, it is also about enabling you to be different—truly different than all the others who do business similar to yours. It takes some thoughtful assessment and strategic actions to establish your brand; however, brand-building is a key strategy for company growth. So, yes— branding is worth it.

SEVEN QUESTIONS TO HELP BUILD YOUR BRAND

Building your brand is critically important to growing your business. As you start working on your brand strategy, here are seven questions to consider:

1. What customer market do you want to serve?
   a. Your market niche
   b. Your position in that market
2. What do the customers in that market value most? In other words, what do they want and need?
3. How do you know?

4. What do you have to do to address the customer's wants and needs?
5. Can you do it? In other words, can you deliver to the customer's satisfaction?
6. How do you do it and ensure consistency?
7. What are the best ways for you to get the word out to create awareness and to generate demand? How do you become remarkable, that is, achieve dominance in the market versus just maintaining competiveness?

And it doesn't matter if you have a small business or even a microbusiness. Microbusinesses grow to be small businesses, and small businesses can grow into larger businesses. Positioning and differentiation count, especially considering the sheer volume of copious and undigested information vying for your attention every day. Ultimately, how will you "rise above the noise"? If you want to stand out in the crowd and grow your business, branding counts.

Branding Starts with Identifying Your Target Market

Your *target market* is the businesses or people you want to serve. Your *market niche* is the subset of the target market where you will concentrate your branding efforts. For example, you may choose health care as your target market and then define rural hospitals as your market niche. This is a critical first step in the branding process, as branding will help build and solidify your market position.

Many entrepreneurs first starting out believe that being as inclusive as possible is the ideal strategy. Their logic is that if they target everyone, they will find out where the strong demand is, and then they can focus on that segment of the market. While seemingly a reasonable concept, it is misguided. Here's why: Being all things to all people (even within your product and service set) is too expensive, spreads your time and focus too thin, and confuses the market. The better strategy is to identify where you want to start, and concentrate your effort and valuable (and oftentimes scarce) resources there.

And to do that, consider the following questions:

- Do you have a high-end product or service, or do you have a commodity?
- Do you want to offer many products or services, or do you want to concentrate on a few?
- Do you want to have a low-volume, high-priced offering, or will you compete on price and target high volume?
- Are you looking for innovators and early adopters, or will you target the late majority and laggards?
- Do you care who your customer is, or do you want to work with only certain people?

These questions begin to frame your target market. Think of this exercise in terms of an upside-down triangle. Initially, you have many options. Then you begin to better define and more clearly focus on whom you want to serve and how you want to serve them.

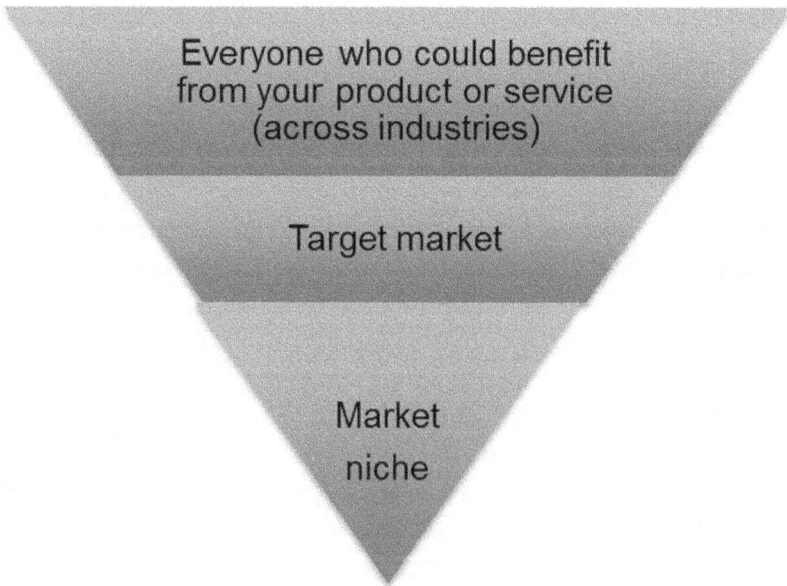

Everyone who could benefit from your product or service (across industries)

Target market

Market niche

One small company in the energy business decided to focus on both the commercial market and the government market. These are two very different markets, with different price sensitivities, different buying processes, and different buying decision timelines. Sales have been slow as a result, and the company has yet to gain traction in either market.

Another company provides software implementation consulting. It decided to focus on one industry (health care), one area within that industry (hospitals), and support one product line. The company's objective is to be the best in the industry. It is, and sales are strong.

Whether you are just starting out or reenergizing your business, defining your target market and the niche within that market will guide your branding strategy.

This is important because your *branding message* must be consistent with your market.

Message consistency is important. Think about the message you send when you do not have an e-mail signature that shows your reader how to reach you. Or if your e-mail address ends in @aol.com, @gmail.com, @yahoo.com, or some other generic e-mail service. With regard to this small detail, we have had people tell us that it doesn't matter. They say what matters is their skills and their ability to do outstanding work. Okay, let's say that's true. Let's say they really do outstanding work. If that's the case, why risk setting up an artificial barrier that may create doubt in the buyer's mind? Remember, the buyer doesn't know you or does not know you well. Why would you want to raise an inconsistency in the buyer's mind?

If you are targeting CEOs as buyers for your services, it is not likely that an aggressive Facebook strategy would be the best approach. LinkedIn would be a better approach. It started as a businessperson's social media tool, while Facebook has been used more for personal connectivity. Also, LinkedIn gives you the opportunity to participate in the same groups that your target client participates in. Through providing thoughtful answers to the questions and statements posed in LinkedIn groups, you have an opportunity to network and add value. You should actively participate in forums where your future customers might be. Your visibility will pique their interest, and you will rise above the usual Internet chatter.

Once, networking was done exclusively face-to-face. And while this is still the preferred method (one reason is that it helps build business relationships), social media sites like LinkedIn provide introductions that can serve as icebreakers, often because you can connect through a mutual connection or professional interest or commonality. When you do finally meet, you already have had an opportunity to share business ideas. But in your responses, you have to position yourself as an intellectual equal and ideally add value—that is, be of assistance to them in some way.

A caveat, however: Don't assume that a social media strategy alone will be successful in attracting business. It won't for the majority of you. We talked with a business owner who wanted to expand his business into a new out-of-state market. He said his strategy was to use social media.

We asked him several questions:

- Who is your target audience?
- How will you add value and get them interested in talking with you?
- Do you have the staff and the resources to serve that market efficiently?
- What will you need (that you don't already have) to serve the market?
- How much time will you (or one of your senior people) spend building relationships with prospective customers in that market?

In other words—what's your strategy, and how does your branding initiative support your strategy?

We told him he didn't have a strategy; he had a tactic, which could or could not be effective, depending on his strategy. Well, needless to say, he never returned our phone calls. This was not what he wanted to hear.

Your target market also drives what you want your communication tools to look like. You, in effect, create an image, an image that supports how you want to be seen and perceived. In the mind of the buyer, perception is reality, and branding helps to establish and reinforce that perception. Since you have a choice, make a strong, positive impression.

BUILDING YOUR BRAND IDENTITY

Building a brand identity is important for any business, and it is especially important for small businesses. Too many small businesses do not invest the time and money to establish a brand.

First is the look and "feel" of the company and what it stands for:

1. Logo
2. Professionally printed business cards (these are not expensive)
    We have our Organizational Gravity model printed on the back of our card and use it as a visual to explain our concept
3. Stationery with your name, physical address, e-mail address, and telephone number on it
4. No handwritten signs or generic store-bought signs (if relevant to your business)—they do not differentiate
5. Electronic signature for all your e-mail correspondence

These are the basics. Everything you send out should present a consistent look and feel about your company. We are not suggesting an expensive branding campaign; we are simply recommending that your business cards, stationery, and website be consistent (i.e., use the same font and same colors). You may be surprised by the number of new start-ups that don't address this issue. You may be even more surprised about how many established business don't address this issue. In the connected world we live in now, these disconnects speak loudly to your virtual network and to your attention to detail.

Second—and perhaps the most powerful tool for branding small businesses these days—is the Internet:

1. Create a website that's interesting and informative. Think of it as a destination site for interesting and informative information rather than as an electronic brochure.
    Include your website address on your business card, stationery, advertisements, and e-mail "signature."
2. Use social networks such as LinkedIn, Google+, Facebook, Twitter, YouTube, etc.(as appropriate for your business model and strategy).
3. Present tips or ideas on how people can benefit from your products and services via a blog or articles posted on your website.

A third powerful, yet often overlooked, contribution to brand-building is how effectively you avoid self-sabotage in your business (i.e., taking time to return calls and e-mails, effectively building relationships, doing what you said you would do when you said you would do it). You can have savvy business cards, the snappiest logo, high-quality stationery, and a compelling website, but if you don't address the intangibles of doing business, these things just won't matter.

Consistency is critical—in appearance, in service, and in performing the intangibles better than your competition.

In addition to the three tips on improving your brand identity, we have four additional points to help you differentiate your business from the competition:

1. Determine your value statement—that is, how do you improve your client or customer's condition? If you don't know or can't articulate it, your clients won't be able to either.
2. Establish your uniqueness (your differentiator) from your key competition and know how to prove it.
3. Identify what your company does best. Consider your service(s) in addition to your products. Also, would your

employees say the same thing? Front-line employees (customer-facing) can support or contradict your message. A worst-case scenario is low employee morale that sabotages the customer relationship.

4. Know and accelerate what makes you different from and better than your competitors, specific to building and maintaining relationships with your clients and customers. (And how do you know? Simply saying it doesn't make it so.)

When you can answer these questions honestly and factually and you have the evidence to support your answers, you have just made a major step forward in differentiating yourself from your competition. Why? Because in our experience, most companies don't bother to truthfully answer these fundamental questions when attempting to build and heighten their brand.

DIFFERENTIATION IS NOT DOING WHAT EVERYONE ELSE IS DOING

Basic marketing tells us to differentiate. Good advice—no, great advice. Then why don't more businesspeople actually do it? Here's what we find: businesspeople say they differentiate, but they really don't. In the business world, we are awash in a sea of sameness, as mentioned in the last chapter. You cannot gain a competitive advantage if you do the same things your competitors are doing. All you can do to be different is lower your price, and that's not a great strategy if you want to be successful.

Differentiation requires thought. You need to define and articulate your value clearly; by that we mean how you, your product, or your service will improve the customer's condition. If you are not clear on it, then neither is your buyer. You need to identify potential buyers who are interested in your value. For most of us this is not broad-based—it's targeted.

In the 2004 presidential election, marketers segmented the voters into distinct buyer personas. This is referred to as "microtargeting" in the political world. In his book, *The New Rules of Marketing and PR*[1], David Meerman Scott provides some examples of microtargeting in the 2004 presidential election. The campaigns targeted "NASCAR Dads" (rural, working-class males, many of whom were NASCAR fans) and "Security Moms" (mothers who were worried about terrorism and concerned about security). They took literally millions of voters, broke them down into microtargets, and designed marketing campaigns that appealed specifically to each group.

Scott mentioned this because it is an excellent concept for the business world as well—especially the small business world.

Differentiation is a powerful tool for all businesses, especially small businesses that face strong competition. Define your value, identify your microtargets, and execute—correcting, modifying, and enhancing along the way.

In thinking further about differentiation, we offer five more steps to get you started:

1. Test your value statement. In other words, do peers and clients agree that it soundly represents you and how they see your business? If so, use it in all your marketing activities. We believe it is best to translate the value statement into a tagline, such as ours: *Helping executives and entrepreneurs build remarkable companies.* Another example from one of our clients is *Making better health care possible.* If your value statement is not well-formed and perceivable when tested, get help defining and refining how you and your product or service will improve your customer's condition or situation.

2. Identify and use a target list (prospective buyers/clients) to guide your marketing and relationship-building activities. Your target list should include in-person contacts, phone calls, e-mails, Internet (through

your website and the number of times your name and your company's name appear in a search), and direct mail options as a means to contact and maintain target and key relationships. Attending business meetings and social events is also a good way to meet future customers.

3. Identify the microtargets within your broader target list. Work to understand why they buy. Two good ways to start are to ask friends who represent your microtarget group or research consumer buying trends on the Internet.

4. Develop a strategy from the above options to identify which ones are best-suited for use within each microtarget group.

5. Then, systematically take action (for example, take three new contacts from your target list and engage in three relationship-building activities per week, per month, whichever is best representative of your target market).

Start by differentiating yourself, your service, and your brand. Build a relationship platform from which clients will get to know you and start buying your products or services. Prospective buyers will begin to find you by reputation. Clients coming to you versus you seeking them out—now that's differentiation.

THE RISK AND COMMONALITY OF BRAND AMBIGUITY

How is your business perceived in the market? When you "show up," is it clear who you are and what you have to offer?

We find that many people just starting out in business—whether as a solopreneur (one-person business) or a small business partnership—have a tendency to want to do too much, too soon. For example, if you provide consulting services to the health care industry, and you tell prospects you can facilitate strategic planning, identify cost-reduction opportunities, conduct employee satisfaction surveys, conduct departmental process improvement studies, and coach executives, it will be difficult for the prospect to truly understand who you are and exactly what you do. And this example doesn't even touch on *where* you would provide these services: at hospitals, physician offices, outpatient facilities, or freestanding surgical centers?

Sure, you can provide all of these services, but who are you and what do you specifically offer? What are you really good at and have the most passion for? It's the difference between going wide and going deep. And going wide is always a harder sell.

We often see this in business start-ups. (We used an example from the health care industry, but we find this in other product and service companies as well.) They believe they can do many things and address many markets. And some have the attitude of "Why should I deprive anyone of all my great products or services?" You shouldn't have this attitude for three reasons:

1. You don't have enough time to cover multiple markets.
2. You don't have the resources to cover multiple markets.
3. You create brand ambiguity.

The purpose of a brand is to be recognized for something in the marketplace— to draw people to you and to create a promise. This is especially important in our interconnected world, where we have the Wild West of competition on the Internet. A market niche is important.

Now, if you are a big enough business, you can provide multiple services to multiple markets. Your brand then becomes a full-service company with "one-stop shopping." But it's a harder sell if you are the single employee in your full-service company!

The temptation is great to go in multiple directions at once. But tempting or not, this is clearly not a good strategy. To take *brand ambiguity* to *brand clarity*, ask yourself the following questions:

- Is your brand clear to your prospects?
- Do they know who you are, what you offer, and your value?

How your business is perceived in the market is a key factor in turning prospects into buyers. While this may seem intuitive, and even obvious, a brand can easily (and unintentionally) become abstruse.

Your brand draws people to you by creating a promise for their improved condition. So, establishing brand clarity begins with aligning who you are (what you do) with a viable market niche. (Note—*viable* is the operative word here. Believe it or not, many overlook this and exuberantly jump into business based only on their passion and neglect understanding and calibrating for the "demand" piece.)

To help you build brand clarity, consider these three techniques:

1. Analyze your market. Conduct a base analysis of your market: who you serve (primary customer), refined into your niche (what specifically do you offer to them); and, lastly, is there market demand (or at least a strong fore-casted opportunity)?

   Understanding what the customers in that market value most will help you refine your niche, your value proposition, and differentiate you from your competition.

2. Establish your brand messages. Ensure your brand messages and touch points (website, marketing materials, etc.) clearly articulate and represent your brand and value proposition.

3. Deliver on your brand promise. Equally important is your ability to consistently deliver on your brand promise (your operations). Otherwise, you are creating a huge and common brand ambiguity, which is saying and doing different things.

The old saying goes, "You can't be all things to all people," and this holds true in business, too. If you do too many things, it's hard to excel, and people may not be able to decipher what it is you do. Hence, the market will overlook you.

PROTECTING YOUR BRAND

Even big companies can make major missteps that create brand ambiguity and confusion in the customer's mind, not to mention a negative reaction from investors.

When HP announced that it was getting out of the PC, tablet, and smartphone business to focus on software, what happened?

The investors got nervous, and many customers were confused. HP, in announcing a major shift in strategy, left the marketplace uncertain (which was reflected in its share price)—never a good thing to do with your business and to your customers.

And it's not only HP that introduced a strategy that left the market confused. Research In Motion (maker of the Blackberry) introduced an upgraded operating system called BB OS7. It was faster and getting some good reviews. But wait—soon after, the company promised its customers that it was upgrading its operating system to QNX in another year, the operating system used on the PlayBook.

Two large companies left the market wondering, "Where do we go from here?" But one thing we do know—its strategy was poorly communicated, and it created brand confusion. A good brand creates clarity. It creates a promise that the customer can count on.

As a small business owner, you need to work diligently not to do this in your market and to your customers. You need to think through your brand (your promise), establish it, and protect it. It's your greatest asset: your differentiator.

Now, depending on the market condition, you may have to change your strategy. And that, in and of itself, is not a bad thing to do. In fact, it can be critical and necessary for the continued growth of the business. So the question for the business owner is not should we change our strategy, but why is change necessary, and how do we protect our brand and use the change as a growth initiative?

Why would you change your strategy? Some reasons include the following:

- The business is no longer growing.
- The market is changing, making your product or service less relevant or irrelevant.

- New market opportunities are opening up that could be more lucrative.

Before you change your strategy, however, it is important to follow these *five steps:*

1. Understand the market—what's changing, why is it changing, and what is the impact on you? This is the analytics part.
2. Define your approach to changing market conditions:
   a. Design a response—your new strategy.
   b. Be sure to clearly define your new target customer base and how you will reach it.
3. Understand the impact your new strategy will have on your current customers:
   a. Will revenue be negatively impacted? (not only in direct sales but also indirect business you get from the customer being your customer)
   b. What will it do to your reputation in the market?
4. Understand how the strategy change will impact your brand:
   a. Will it reinforce your current brand?
   b. Will you need to re-brand?
5. Explain, explain, explain—talk to your customers and communicate with your staff.

As we have stated over and over, your brand is your promise to the market. It's how customers (and prospects) see you and know you. If your brand is providing highly personalized customer service, rapid response, and attentiveness, your brand will likely still apply as you change your strategy. If your brand is very specific to your current strategy (for example, we provide computers, and now we are moving away from providing computers), then you will need to re-brand along with developing your new strategy—and you need to do it at the same time.

Customer focus and customer knowledge are critically important to your business. Know your customers and the impacts of any changes you make on your customers.

THE PLACEBO EFFECT AND YOUR BUSINESS

We've all heard of the placebo effect. The phrase is most often used to describe a perceived or actual improvement after a course of treatment that in and of itself has no therapeutic value. It's when a belief creates a result where no clear cause-and-effect relationship exists. One lesson the placebo effect teaches us is that our perceptions can drive our reality, for example, when a "sugar pill" causes a reduction in blood pressure.

What we learn from the placebo effect is that there is more involved in creating results (i.e., effects) than the facts or the science. Facts—tangible/measurable events alone—do not create outcomes. There is an intangible, emotional factor that helps create outcomes. This lesson can be applied to your business.

Buyers make decisions based on emotion, not on facts alone. Why do you choose the car you choose? Why do you decide to do business with one person and not another? Why does the luxury market exist and thrive? Facts?—Unlikely. Do you need the facts? Most definitely. But research shows we make decisions emotionally.

How are you creating an emotional appeal for your buyer? How are you filling the space left open once the facts are consumed? Whether you do this, and how you do this, supports and grows your brand. If buyers believe, based on your brand, that you provide high-quality, personalized, and caring service, that's how you will be perceived. That's how your reputation will develop. The facts most definitely should support your brand, but the buying decision will be made on that intangible, perceived value.

Here are some ideas on how you can create a greater emotional appeal for your buyers.

1. Are you creating and presenting a "likeable and approachable" image to the market? You may be smart as can be, but if you are not approachable and likeable, you're at a disadvantage. (This has to do with your brand—your

image, message, and delivery. People tend to buy from people they like.) True, we see some contrarian behavior (that is, people who are dismissive and can appear to some as rude)—but the successful salespeople do so in an emotive way. This takes careful balance between being personal (and interesting enough to pay attention to) and having the business sense and success that draw people to you.

2. Fundamentals are great, but do you have a handle on the up-and-coming? Are you knowledgeable of economic and market changes, demographics, trends, and technology? It is a beautifully diverse world these days—are you staying abreast of it so as to sufficiently calibrate your own business and best respond to your customers' needs? In other words, are you helping your customers envision a better future with your product or service—a future grounded in developing trends?

3. Don't hide. If you do, you quickly become invisible and the "noise" of others takes over. Be visible, stand up in the crowd, and be willing to speak for what you believe in; otherwise, you won't be noticed. This includes tooting your own horn when appropriate.

4. Always, always, always have the buyers' best interests in mind. Buyers buy based on emotion, but if the emotion was triggered through deceit, buyer's remorse will soon set in, and you become someone who won't be trusted. And in this highly connected world, word spreads.

ARE YOU MANAGING YOUR COMPANY'S REPUTATION? AVOID DAMAGE CONTROL

There once was a time when reputation (good or bad) was carried by word of mouth. Remember the aphorism (we're paraphrasing here), "Receive good service and one person knows; receive bad service and ten of your friends know." Well, we have news for you. In 2012, you should be so lucky to have only ten people know if you provided bad service to a customer. In today's interconnected world, give bad service and the world may know, literally, within minutes.

If you are inclined to doubt this, look at the impact social media had in Egypt, or the reaction to the Susan G. Komen Foundation's decision to withdraw support from Planned Parenthood.

In Egypt, some pundits (who dubbed it "The Twitter Revolution") argued that organizers spread the word on how to organize and where to show up through Twitter messaging: rapid and literally instant communication. Now some have argued that the Internet and Twitter played a small, if not insignificant, role in the Egyptian revolution. But the reality of instant communication is very real and becoming a major force in spreading opinions, thoughts, and reactions.

The Susan G. Koman Foundation decided to withdraw support of Planned Parenthood. The online storm was swift and strong, resulting in the foundation withdrawing its decision.

Now, within this terrifying potential of exposure and influence lies tremendous power for the entrepreneur—reputation management. That's right—you have an opportunity to manage how prospective customers see you. It's better than the Yellow Pages; it's better than word of mouth; and it's better than advertising. And best of all—it's free.

Your reputation is being framed by services collectively called social directories. These include Angie's List, InsiderPages, JudysBook, ServiceMagic, and Zipingo. These services are set up to capture word of mouth wisdom. Consumers submit reviews of the service they received and post them on the sites. Additionally, social networking sites (such as Facebook and LinkedIn) elicit recommendations, and Twitter promotes tweets, good and bad. People with access to these sites (which is most of us these days) can read the reviews and make purchasing decisions accordingly.

Now, instead of musing about how people would flock to your company and happily buy your service if they only knew how good you were, you have a way to make that happen.

We have a special interest in working with women entrepreneurs and enjoyed the story published on January 1, 2010, in *Angie's List* about three businesswomen who carved out a niche for themselves in the male-dominated contracting field. It relates the story of these "highly rated service providers" who pursued careers once performed exclusively by men. Quality counts in the mind of the buyer—regardless of gender, race, or age.

How many times have you heard (or may have even said yourself)—I'm too old, I'm too young, I'm the wrong gender, and so on, ad nauseam. For the vast majority of professions and business, it doesn't matter. What matters is how good you are at what you do and more importantly, who says so.

You can manage your reputation by

- providing outstanding service;
- encouraging written testimonials (including testimonials on the social directories);
- improving your service if the feedback you get suggests how you can improve;
- ensuring that you let your prospective customers know where they can find reviews of your work.

You can catapult yourself and your company to growth and profitability faster than at any time in the past by knowing how to manage your reputation. And there is nothing manipulative about it. You provide valuable work, and thousands of people learn about it. There is nothing wrong with claiming it—in fact, you should. To use a title from one of Wayne Dyer's books, *excuses begone.*

PART THREE

CULTURE

CHAPTER

5

CULTURE

Once you've identified your market (customer and audience) and your message (brand strategy and expression) you want to send into the market, it's time to deliver. The brand serves as the attractor for your talent—it gets the attention of future employees. But the culture draws them in and keeps them in. And it's the company (or organizational) culture—that creates and ensures delivery.

WHAT IS CULTURE?

Culture is the "way work is done around here." It reflects shared values, beliefs, and attitudes, as demonstrated through behavior. It's seen in how people work together and heard by what they say; it's how you build your teams, infrastructure, and processes to deliver on your promise. It's how you lead, manage, develop, and implement strategy. It represents how strongly you believe in your promise, and it builds your reputation.

Culture is grounded in the understanding and common practices around the mission, vision, and values of the company. It drives how decisions are made and how responsibility is assumed, and it determines your behavior in front of customers and within your group. It is reflected in the standards and consistency with which you deliver your product or service. Culture will either foster or hinder your goals and outcomes.

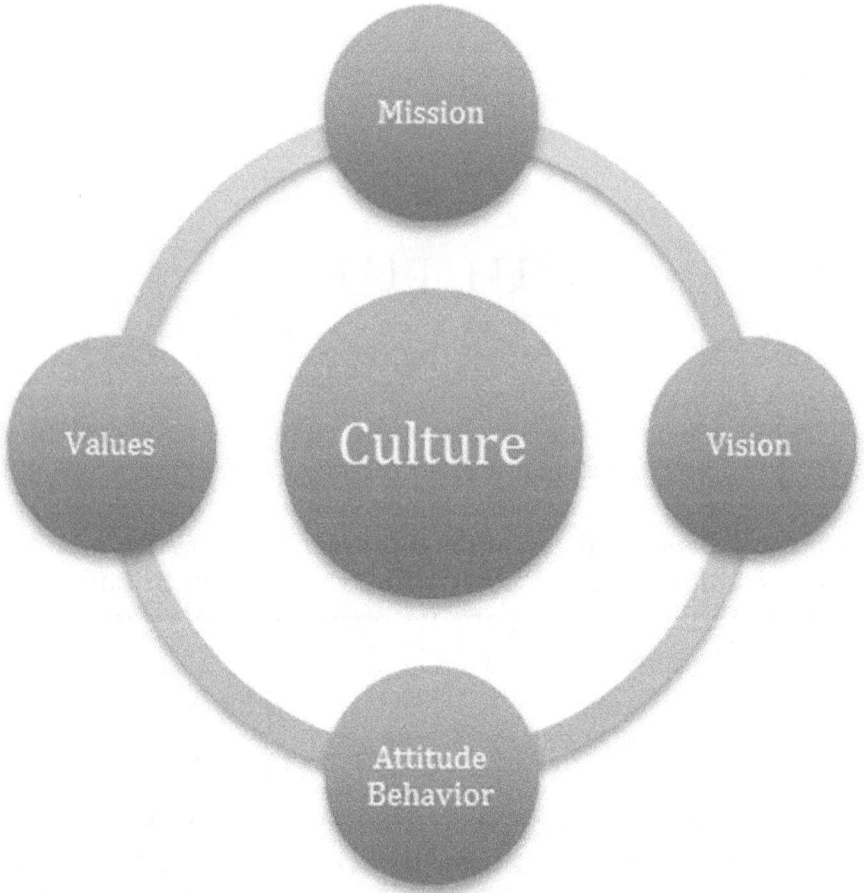

Unfortunately, some business owners and executives still believe that addressing culture is a waste of time. They're not about to start pampering people. They have real work to get done—work that will increase revenue, work that can be tracked and measured by statistics such as revenue, gross profit, market share, and so forth. These are the "hard matters of business," they tell us. Well, we are not about to start challenging the need for business metrics and business strategy. What we will challenge, however, is the belief that culture (and culture-building) is a waste of time.

Ideally, what business owners and leaders should realize is that today, right now, in your business, your culture is alive. Yet you may argue that you did nothing about creating a culture, so how can that be a true statement? Culture arises whether you like it or not. It forms out of the nature of group dynamics—standards, relationships, and norms (behavior). And your culture will either support attracting and retaining customers and top talent, or it won't.

THE INFORMAL ORGANIZATION

You have most likely heard of the "informal" organization. The informal organization includes subgroups that employees form (i.e., cliques or support groups), and it directs how work gets done. The informal organization serves as a conduit for the informal communication channel and creates a "reaction panel" to the initiatives management introduces. This group sometimes has no formal leader, or if it does, it is often a person who is very influential (usually charismatic) and not associated with management. The informal organization is a powerful influence on work and relationships within an organization. And if a negative leader leads it, it becomes a "shadow organization" and largely operates underground and behind the scenes.

Informal organizations will either work to attract and serve customers well, or not. It will accept or reject new candidates and new ideas and direction from management. In essence, it serves as the organization's immune system, fending off "pathogens" that the system believes will harm it. The irony is, if the informal organization works counter to the goals and intent of the formal organization, this "immune response" will

slowly kill off the intended—but left unattended—formal organization. In biological terms, the organization has an autoim-
mune disease.

So, it really doesn't matter what you think *about* culture. The
key point is that you have one. The important question is, is it a
positive culture, or is it a negative one?

Your organization should take the following steps:

- Assess your culture to understand whether it is supporting or impeding growth.
- Determine what you need your culture to be to deliver
  your brand promise.
- Do something about it. Take action to strengthen your
  company culture, starting with embedding meaningful mission/purpose, vision, and value statements in
  your organization to build shared attitudes, beliefs, and
  behaviors to drive performance and outcomes.

A common challenge is for existing organizations to align their
informal organization with the mission, vision, and values of the
formal organization, so they can move the organization forward
in a unified, positive direction. And if the formal organization has
no identified mission, vision, or values—or if it has them, and
they are irrelevant, unknown, or not practiced—this is where
the shadow organization will emerge. While new companies
have many challenges upon start up, at least they have the
opportunity to develop their formal organization and drive
culture from the beginning. Then, it is simply a matter of the
executives and leaders making sure there is ongoing relevancy
in the company's stated mission, vision, and values and that
their people's attitudes, behaviors, and outcomes reflect it.

Consider this metaphor on sailing: ignoring your culture
while working to build and implement a growth strategy is like
trying to sail a boat without a keel. Sure, the boat can sail, but
it's unstable. Difficult weather conditions (read: challenging economic times) can and often do capsize the boat, even though
everything above the surface seems to be fine.

PUTTING CULTURE IN PERSPECTIVE

Are organizations with a strong, positive culture and good brand expression perfect? Far from it; they are just better than their competition because they know why they exist as a business. They have better alignment within their organization to drive organizational performance than the individuals who make it up. They know how to course-correct when something does not work well or as expected. They can fix the issue, and they often fix it quickly.

It's like the story of the two hikers walking in the woods. As they turn the corner, they see a clearing. In the clearing, lumbering around a downed tree, is a bear. The first hiker turns to the other and says, "Do you think we can outrun the bear?" The second hiker says, "It doesn't matter." The perplexed first hiker questions, "What do you mean it doesn't matter? That bear can kill us." The second hiker clarifies, "It doesn't matter if we can outrun the bear; what matters is whether I can outrun you."

You need to "outrun" your competition, and the quality and strength of your culture will help you do just that.

So, culture is not the soft stuff that many believe it is. It drives how decisions are made, how responsibility is assumed, your behavior in front of customers and within your group, and the standards and consistency with which you deliver your product or service.

While your brand sets the promise, your culture drives your ability to deliver on that promise. One of the worst things you can do is to make a promise and not deliver on it. Do not say the empty words we are all too familiar with, such as "Your call is very important to us—please leave a detailed message, and we will get right back with you." Yet, days later, the call that was "so important" has still not been returned.

Or when you promise a deliverable, such as completing a project on time and within budget, yet the experience is something different and disappointing. Is the response an apology or an excuse? How many times have you heard, "This has never happened before" or "I just don't know what to say"?

When the promise (brand) is not met, you have two choices: (1) Own it, apologize, and swiftly fix it; or (2) Make excuses, deflect, and blame. How you respond smacks of your culture.

Remember the advertisement Wendy's put out in the 1980s with the grandmotherly actor looking at a fluffy bun, and saying, with more than a hint of dissatisfaction and crankiness, "Where's the beef?"

Well, customers, future customers, and prospective employees will do the same thing to you. You can't serve up a "fluffy bun"; you need to serve up the beef.

CUSTOMERS EXPECT YOU TO DELIVER

Remember, customers come to you and stay with you because there is something about you and your business that works for them. As mentioned in the branding chapter, it could be they like dealing with high-end companies, or it could be that they like your price and convenience. What matters is they get from you what they expect.

Yet what's surprising is that many organizational cultures support (either actively or through inattention)

- insensitive treatment
- poor responsiveness
- poor delivery
- excuses.

We hear business owners argue that they do not tolerate such treatment, yet it goes on every day.

Let's think about why this happens. You have a limited amount of cash to spend, and you have choices on how you want to spend it. You can, for example,

- improve your branding initiative
- increase executive pay/bonuses
- improve technology.

But since you have a finite pool of money, spending in one area requires you to take from (or not invest in) another area. One place some businesses take from is employee compensation and perks. So what happens? In the employees' perception, what they believe the culture says is, "We (management) really don't care about you, the employee; we have more important things to invest in.—You understand, don't you?" Well, they don't.

What you've created is disgruntled employees; you've reinforced a culture that is not all that concerned with the employees; and you have also created the ingredients for poor service. The one thing a company wants to do is attract and retain customers, and ironically, what you end up doing is creating a force within the company that repels customers.

Culture is that obscure force. And it is powerful.

You've Brought Talent to the Door—Now What?

Future employees need to be excited about what they see when they meet you. If they see any of the following issues, your message will not be positive:

- an interviewer who is late for the interview;
- an interviewer who is unprepared;
- an interviewer who talks negatively about other interviewers the candidate will be meeting;
- an interviewer who complains about a lack of support from the executive group or from other departments;
- a somber atmosphere within the company;
- excuses, such as "We are really busy, you understand; we'll get to you as soon as we can—thanks for understanding." (Note: what the prospective employee hears is, "We are so disorganized and out of control; we can't even keep an appointment.")

Candidates, especially "high-potential and top talent," want to have their expectations met. They want to see and hear

- excitement about where the company is going;
- frequent talk about the team and "how we get things done";
- success stories and "how we win in the marketplace";
- stories about the successes of employees, both in a job-related context and in a personal/community context;
- well-prepared and interested interviewers;
- on-time meetings.

None of this costs money! All are the by-products of a company with a strong culture.

Now ask yourself this question: Do you know the experience prospective employees and interviewees have with your company?

If you want to compete effectively for scarce talent and continue to grow your company, you better know.

KNOWING YOUR CULTURE

So how is your culture? If you don't know—ask. Here's a potent way to do it: Conduct a climate or employee satisfaction and engagement survey that combines a standardized electronically administered questionnaire and interviews with a randomly selected group of employees across all levels of your organization.

Can this be the source of some concern? Of course. Some business executives couldn't care less what their employees think; some don't want to hear the answers; and some are afraid the exercise will be disruptive and "put ideas in employees' heads" about how their work environment (or their supervisors) could, and should, improve.

Yes, gaining this knowledge can be daunting, and yes, it can be a little intimidating. But you can't change what you don't know. So if you are happy with the results you are getting, then by all means keep doing what you're doing. But if you are not, then you need to think differently. Remember, the definition of insanity is doing the same things over and over again and expecting different results.

If you choose to conduct a climate survey (which we recommend to business owners and leaders), we strongly advise that you not hold the survey results "close to the vest," keeping them only to yourself or members of the senior executive team. Secrecy, by the way, is another sign of a weak culture. The results from the survey and interviews should be presented first to the full executive team along with an analysis of findings and a listing of what the employees believe would improve their experience at your company. The leader must not tolerate excuses, explanations, or pleas to remove certain information because it is embarrassing to a group or because "the employees really don't understand what we are trying to do around here." Oh, they do. It's the one who spouts a statement like that who doesn't really understand.

After you review the information, understand what the employees are saying to you and act on it—including sharing the results and your plan with the employees.

We suggest that fundamental climate survey questions should explore

- the employees' clarity of the company's mission (purpose), vision, and values;
- how they see the company's priorities (or strategic goals);
- what they think is going well;
- what could go better;
- specific questions about performance accountability, teamwork, trust in leadership, internal relationships, compensation and benefits, motivation and other factors that directly relate to them and to their satisfaction and engagement with the company.

Follow-up and transparency are important to help employees feel you care and are acting upon their feedback. Miss this, and next time they won't engage, and skepticism will grow.

Remember, it is the business owner and key executives who define the culture (or should define the culture). In other words, you should set the example of how you expect "work to be done around here" and what values you think are important for the company (values that *you* live every single day—not values you think your employees should live every single day). The informal organization notices and responds to whether or not you and the executive team live the values that you set.

Remember, as your candidate travels through your organization (or over the airways in a virtual company), the issues that are revealed in a climate survey will also be seen and experienced by the candidate. What they observe will either reinforce a culture of caring about employees, or it will punctuate the last sentence in the recruitment script and have the candidate mutter "the end."

THE CULTURE AND TALENT INTERRELATIONSHIP

We talked with a business owner who developed a unique product for the petroleum, chemical, and grain industries. He has successfully completed a proof of concept; he has interested buyers; and he is preparing to go to market as of this writing. What he needs, however, are a few highly talented engineers. He further defined his ideal candidate: a skilled engineer with about ten years of experience who will accept a lateral move for three to five years.

We asked him, what makes you special? Why would a successful mid-career engineer take a lateral move to work for you? His answer was intriguing. He said that if someone did, when he sold the company (which was his three- to five-year objective), his written commitment to each one of the engineers would be to write him or her a seven-figure check. Now that is a compelling proposition and surely will get the attention of highly talented engineers who have a higher tolerance for risk than their colleagues.

Another business was a start-up service company in a highly competitive technology market. Resources were in high demand, and competition was becoming more intense each month with "mom and pop" companies entering this lucrative market. The competition for resources was also intense, and represented a serious growth-limiting factor.

The business had options: It could pay more than its competitors and hence charge its clients more (or accept a lower margin), or it could create a work environmént where people wanted to work; in effect, draw talent to them. The latter option was more challenging and had a longer timeline. But it also had an advantage: people who came to work for this company tended to stay longer due to its desirable culture.

The company embarked on its culture-building strategy and started with a climate survey to assess its current state. It was quite positive, but the company was still young, and many of its employees had been handpicked by the executives to join the company. They had worked with each other in the past and already had a positive relationship.

When the climate survey was conducted again a year later, the company had grown over one hundred percent. The "familiarity" factor was dissipating, as new hires no longer had past business relationships with the executives. What happened was interesting. The overall satisfaction with working for the company improved on all elements measured except for one: comfort with talking with the executives. This was not surprising and provided an early warning sign about the need for management to maintain contact with its growing workforce. Actions have been taken to address this issue.

By the way, this company was named one of Modern Healthcare's 100 best places to work for 2012.

KNOWING/DOING

If you are not assessing the climate within your organization, and you are frustrated with turnover and the inability to find qualified candidates, realize that it's your decision (or lack of it).

Just don't waste other people's time complaining about the lack of qualified candidates. People like to work with good people; they like to enjoy their work environment; they like and deserve to feel good about whom they work for—both the company and the boss. And this comes when you marry a positive brand with a positive culture. You can't improve what you choose not to notice.

BRAND + CULTURE = MARKET GROWTH

Without a strong base (your culture and brand), delivering consistent and high-quality products and services to your market is nearly impossible. (In this case, what you end up delivering is excuses and uncertainty.)

Earlier, we discussed RIM and its rapid deterioration in the marketplace. We initially introduced the company in the branding section, but missing so badly in the marketplace is a cultural issue. The company's problems were many:

- how executives developed strategy
- how they saw their competition
- how honest they were with the information coming in about their competition
- how well they solicited feedback and listened to their employees
- how they reacted to the changing conditions in the market
- how willing they were to change their approach.

These are cultural issues. Was it a culture of complacency, or was it a culture of arrogance?

In the end, it was a company that could not run as fast as Apple and the new Android smartphones, and you know what happens to the slowest runner.

What could the co-CEOs have done to avoid being outmaneuvered in the marketplace? They should have

- recognized that the market for smartphones was changing from corporate use to consumer use—and consumer use was entering businesses;
- evolved its culture to encourage openness, suggestions, ideas, and innovation—and listen to the input invited;
- created an environment where apps could be written for the Blackberry;
- replaced the co-CEO structure, since it likely slowed critical decision-making;
- delivered on its promise to introduce a new operating system.

The cultural lesson learned from RIM is important. It contributed to the downfall of a once-market leader.

Companies with a strong brand and a strong culture are leaders in their market, whether it's a small, local market or a large, international market. It doesn't matter. *A positive brand and cultural alignment is a powerful competitive strategy!*

Identifying your market and building a strong base (culture and brand) to deliver to that market is a *competitive differentiator*. Why? Because many of your competitors (and would-be competitors) do not take the time to do this. And prospective talent and your clients and customers will notice, which provides you with an advantage.

CHAPTER

6

CULTURE SUPPLEMENT: A SERIES OF TIPS AND TECHNIQUES TO FOSTER CULTURE BUILDING

CULTURE AND BRAND — THE BEDROCK OF BUSINESS GROWTH

It's one thing to make a promise; it's quite another to keep it. Yet businesses make promises every day. Some keep them; some have good intentions but can't keep them. And worst of all, some businesses have no sincere intention of keeping them at all, regardless of what they say.

How are you and your business at keeping your promises? Well, how you answered this question just defined your *brand* and your *culture*. Yes, the two are connected, and this connection can be either

- strong and reinforcing—they are in alignment;
- strong, but negatively reinforcing—they are competing or demonstrating dissonance;
- weak—they have not been defined and developed.

CREATING THE PROMISE — YOUR BRAND

As we have already written about brand in chapters 3 and 4, to grow your business, you must identify your target market, the market niche you want to focus on, and the position you want to hold within that market. You need to know and understand exactly what products or services you want to provide to your market. You need to know what you can do and what you do not want to do; you need to know your competition and why you are different. This knowledge provides the essential elements for branding your company.

Branding presents you to the marketplace. It defines you in the mind of your customers and prospects. *It creates the promise*: what your clients can expect from you when they do business with you. Think of Apple, Google, Zappos, Amazon.com, and Nordstrom—we know what to expect from them, and we are rarely disappointed.

Branding expresses this promise in the company's logo; its website concept and content; its tagline, advertisements, marketing materials; and all forms of internal and external expression/communication about the company. There is a consistency that carries over to all methods of interacting with the customer and the prospect. Oftentimes, you can be recognized by the colors and symbols alone that you use to represent your company. And put together, all of this provides the promise.

Regardless of how your prospective and existing customers enter your sales cycle, they will see, feel, and interpret who you are, what you stand for, and what they can expect, based on your branding.

So, you've got their attention with relevant and compelling branding.

You're done, right? No—not so quickly.

CREATING THE CULTURE TO DELIVER THE PROMISE

Now it's time to deliver: to keep the promise made in and through your branding.

As we described in chapter 5, culture is the *way work is done* in your company. It's how people work together; it's how you build your teams and processes to deliver on your promise. And it represents how strongly you believe in your promise.

Culture is grounded in the understanding and practices around the purpose/mission, vision, and guiding values of the company. It drives how decisions are made, how responsibility is assumed, your behavior in front of customers and within your group, and the standards and consistency with which you deliver your product or service.

One quick point we want to reinforce: are organizations with a strong positive culture and good brand expression perfect? Far from it. They are just much better than their competition, as they know how to course-correct when required, and they know why they exist as a business.

Brand + Culture = Market Growth

Think of brand, culture, and market growth as a triangle. On top, you have the *market*, where you are "pointing" your efforts. The two bottom blocks that establish your base are *culture* and *branding*. Without a strong base, it is impossible to deliver consistently high-quality products and services to your market. (In this case, what you end up delivering is excuses.)

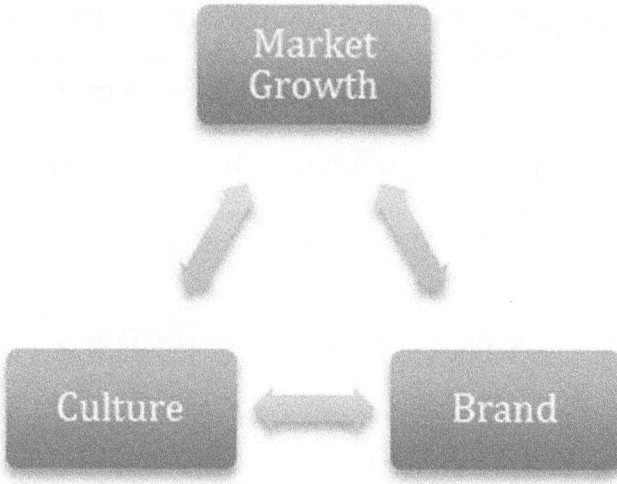

Companies with a strong brand and a strong culture are leaders in their markets, whether it's a small, local market, or a large, international market. It doesn't matter. A positive brand coupled with cultural alignment is a powerful competitive strategy!

Yet, there are still companies that have strong brands and strong cultures that do not always "wow" the customer. Think of AT&T, US Airways, and Bank of America. They consistently rank low in customer satisfaction. Their strong brands and strong cultures are *not* aligned.

Many companies we see have both a weak brand and a weak culture—some because they are new and some because they have simply not understood the importance of brand and culture to profitability and growth. Remember, all companies have a culture; it develops naturally within an organization. But one that develops on its own lacks the power and focus to enhance business growth and is often informal or even negative in nature. This type of culture also always exists within an environment of poor leadership.

Identifying your market and building a strong base (culture and brand) to deliver to that market is a *competitive differentiator.* Why? Because many of your competitors (and would-be competitors) will not take the time to do this. Believe us when we say your clients and customers will notice and will reward your efforts.

CONSISTENCY BUILDS CULTURE AND ENABLES GROWTH

We spoke with a manager who told us she had eight different bosses over a three-year period—this company was experiencing high employee turnover.

We spoke with a middle manager who told us that unless he hears a request from his boss at least three times, he will not respond. This company changes key initiatives frequently—both small initiatives (division-level) and big initiatives (company-level). The changes are not showing up in company growth.

We spoke with another middle manager who told us that the CEO was hiring executives from outside the company, and the practice was destroying the culture—performance has not improved in this company, and some of the newly hired executives were terminated or left in less than two years.

What do these three stories have in common? What they have in common is lack of consistency within the organizations. These examples demonstrate a more insidious and harmful impact on the organization than the oft-spoken "flavor of the month" behavior of some senior executives and CEOs. The "flavor of the month" is actually a pejorative term applied to constantly changing initiatives, organizational focus, and urgent needs.

Employees like consistency. One reason is that it provides for predictability. Another reason is that it helps them develop influence that, in turn, helps them get work done more efficiently and effectively. Influence, however, develops in organizations over time and can only develop and take hold in organizations where there is management consistency.

Many managers foolishly believe that constant change is good. Some change is good; frequent change is not. Bring in a new manager, and what's one of the first things that he or she does? Reorganize. Bring in enough new managers, and the organization begins to feel it's in a constant state of reorganization and destabilization. Whether you take issue with this and don't believe it, it doesn't matter. What matters is how the employees perceive it because they act on their perceptions, not on management's statements or beliefs. And what also matters is the metrics—revenue growth (supported by a strong and growing contribution margin), employee retention, and other metrics that demonstrate strong performance results.

Lack of consistency by you and among your management and departments will have an insidious and harmful impact on your organization. So, there are two elements to consider here: consistency within yourself (your words and behaviors shown in your actions) and consistency across your company/organization, which begins or ends with your management.

We start with some thoughts for you as an individual leader. While basic in nature, unfortunately, these are often not practiced regularly, resulting in waning consistency.

1. Do what you agreed to—in other words, do what you said you would do, on time.
    a. If you can't meet the agreement/expectation, surface it and renegotiate as soon as you are aware of it. And apologize, if appropriate!
2. Choose wisely what you commit to do—overcommitting equals not being able to keep your word, which smacks of inconsistency.
3. As a leader/manager, be fair and equitable to your subordinates, as inconsistency in your actions resonates as favoritism and lack of caring.
4. Ask for feedback from someone you trust on how well you are matching what you say with what you do. Your actions trump your words.

Next, work toward consistency in and across your organization:

1. This begins with you individually and one-on-one with your employees, as defined above.
2. Establish clear standards and practices, policies, systems, and protocols to guide consistency across divisions and departments.

3. Train and reinforce with your management team; identify organizational standards and practices, and align them across the organization. (Be especially careful to ensure new managers are grounded in your organizational standards and practices before they start to lead and manage.)
4. Communicate in multiple ways—both verbally and in writing—the company's standards and practices so employees are clear about what to expect. Communication needs to be constant; look for opportunities to reinforce your message.

Consistency is an intangible that when practiced leads to a stronger, more vibrant, and more successful organization. It is difficult for anyone to perform well if he or she sees inconsistency in behavior, performance, and expectations.

CULTURE — MADE BY INTENTION AND FILLED WITH STORIES

When we talk with business owners about the importance of culture and how it drives business results, we get a wide array of responses. Some tell us they know how important culture is and explain how they send this message to their employees, but they are the rare exceptions.

Mostly, we hear the opposite:

- Culture is that soft stuff—I've got no time for touchy-feely in my business.
- I can't spend time on culture—I've got too many things going on right now that are more important to the success of my business.
- What can I do about culture? It is what it is.
- You can't change culture.
- You don't introduce culture into an organization; it just develops on its own.

Well, every one of these points (and opinions) is missing something. Most often we hear them from business owners who do not understand the power of culture. You will either define your culture, or it will define you. And when it does, you may not like what you see.

Developing, changing, or reinforcing your business's culture is less about time and more about intention and stories. Every day you communicate to your staff—you communicate by words, actions, decisions, and behavior. You are either consistent with your values, or you are not. You either reinforce the mission, vision, and values of your company, or you do not. None of what we just mentioned takes time—you are doing it anyway. It is how you do it and how you reinforce "the way work will be done around here."

And telling stories about how individuals in your organization improved service, or how an effort made your customer's life better, or how the company's values were demonstrated is a living example of your culture. It's about intention—intentionally and frequently communicating and reinforcing what defines your organization.

Culture gains life through stories. Stories have power. People love to hear stories. Stories make the message feel genuine and relevant.

For example, a senior executive in your company holds a division meeting and says, "We want to thank you for the good work you are doing with our clients. Jim, Sue, Frank—thank you for your work you did with ABC Company; it was appreciated by the client.—Good job. It looks like we may get the next phase."

Contrast the above message with this version:

> Everyone, I want to take a quick moment to recognize three of you today—Jim, Sue, and Frank. I got a call just this morning from Jack MacDonald. As you know, Jack is the president of ABC Company. He called to tell me about the outstanding job Jim, Sue, and Frank did on the current project we are doing for him. Jack's back was against the wall, and the three of you stepped up and bailed him out. He couldn't say enough positive things

about you. And, as you know, Jim was the project lead and Sue and Frank aren't assigned to this project. But they stepped up to give Jim a hand—and as they say—the rest is history. Oh, and, by the way, Jack started talking about having us do the next phase of the project, which as we all know is the largest phase. Thank you... all of you. It's cooperation like this that makes everything work around here.

Both messages communicated basically the same idea: three people did a good job, the client was pleased, and it looks like is the company will be awarded more work. But one was given as a report; the other told a story. Which one do you think will have the biggest impact?

In our experience, stories serve to build and sustain a culture. And it doesn't take any more time to tell a story than it does to give a report. Yet, the difference in impact on your company is huge.

THE POWER IN WORDS

You've heard it before: words have power. Words have the power to motivate, the power to energize, the power to call to action, and the power to disappoint.

As in politics, people want to believe the words, yet quickly become disenchanted when the actions don't match the words. We frequently say, based on continuous proof, behavior trumps words.

Businesses are looking for an opportunity to grow again. Yet some don't fully appreciate or acknowledge that the business landscape has changed; they are still using the old rhetoric buttressed by pre-recession beliefs. For others, it's a ripe opportunity for success, and they have found a way to communicate it not only to their employees, but also to the marketplace. It is about your words, and more deeply, your beliefs that fuel them.

As a business leader, you should take three actions:

1. Tell your employees how business will get better, how you will grow, and how the workplace will return to a "new normal."
2. Hold planning meetings to identify a future state for the business and identify what is required to get to that future state. We highly recommend you engage your employees at some level in your strategy work.
3. Based on the above, identify an implementation plan with timelines and accountabilities, and take action that matches your words.

Words without actions are disempowering, disappointing, and demoralizing. You, as the leader, have complete control over the message—how it's delivered and how you make it real. Behavior, whether individual or organizational, becomes controversial, incongruent, or superficial at best when it does not align with your statements. Consistency is important: consistency in the message and consistency in the actions that support the message. As a leader, what message do you want to be known for?

There are two critical ingredients to communicating effectively with employees: what you say and what you do.

Neither stands alone. Words without action are either lies or false promises; actions without words fall short of effective communication because actions alone are open to interpretation—some of which may not be favorable, based on the perceiver.

Writer Ralph Waldo Emerson once said, "What you do speaks so loudly I can't hear what you say?" And this is as relevant today as when he wrote it in the nineteenth century.

Effective communication starts with well-thought-out (intentional) words that frame your intended message. And equally important to what you say is *how* you say it (your tone and corresponding body language) and how often you say it, if it needs to be a reinforced message.

For example, if you want to get your team to focus on improving your contribution margin, you must

- explain what you want to do (the "what" factor);
- explain why you want to do it—what the company stands to gain (the "so what" factor);
- discuss risks and consequences of not doing it ("if/then" factor);
- provide examples of how it can be done and any relevant guidelines ("now what" and "what's next" factors).

Then you must repeat this message in meetings (both group and one-on-one), in conversations with employees, and in your newsletter, e-mails, and other forms of internal communications. We often tell our clients that when you are tired of saying the same thing over and over again, the staff is just beginning to hear you. Exaggerated? Perhaps a little, but less than you may think.

Three general tips to empowerment language:

1. Be focused and concise in your use of words—don't use filler language ("fluff") or ramble on with unnecessary stories. And, by all means, do not drift into different issues.
2. Be honest and transparent (hidden agendas will surface and create distrust). And if you don't know something yet, say so.
3. Stay on the "high road" with appropriate, professional, respectful, and courteous word choices—simply stated, be neutral or positive versus negative in your word selection to reduce defensiveness in your audience and the chance you may potentially offend someone.

In addition to your words, you must take action. You must identify actions that will achieve the desired result (i.e., improve contribution margin), and then implement those actions. And as the leader, you, personally, cannot make exceptions for you or your team; you must lead from the front. You must be taking actions every day to demonstrate ways to improve the contribution margin. Talk about it and reinforce it through words and consistency in your behavior.

It's like a circle. You explain what you want to do and why you want to do it. You do it. And then you reinforce through words what you've done and explain it again.

If you behave like we described above, your future words will have more power and more meaning because it will become clear to your employees that you mean what you say.

THE LANGUAGE OF BUSINESS

You can find a wealth of information about how a business runs and how well it does with its employees and customers simply by listening to the words the leaders use.

Words create perception; perception creates a perceived reality; and a perceived reality drives behavior. And behavior has consequences, by either reinforcing or deteriorating relationships. [Tip: One of our favorite business books explores this principle in great detail. It's called *Tribal Leadership, Leveraging Natural Groups to Build a Thriving Organization*[1].]

Listen to the words used in your organization. Do you hear these phrases?

- "Our CEO is incompetent."
- "This place sucks—we have no chance to do what we want."
- "The customer has no idea what he wants."
- "People around here just aren't making the grade; no wonder we're behind our competition."
- "The problem with some of our people is they're not ready for prime time."
- "The only person you can trust is yourself—everyone's out for his or her own back."

Or do you hear phases like these?

- "Our customers are amazing and remarkably loyal."
- "If it wasn't for this team, there would be no way we could have finished this project."

- "We have so many good people; no wonder we are doing so well."
- "Our problem is that we are growing fast, which is a good problem to have."
- "Our CEO actually gave his cell phone number out, and we are all welcome to call him if we have a concern."
- "This is such a great place to work. The staff loves it here, and our customers love doing business with us."

Look at the words used—customer, employee, CEO—similar words; very different descriptions. And how these descriptions are used and how regularly will largely influence your culture—and thereby your employees' experiences, the customers' experiences, and ultimately, your profitability!

As the leader, CEO, president, or business owner, you have a responsibility to set the example and shape the culture of the organization—and one key way you do this is through your use of language.

And if you happen to think that how you use language is not all that important, you can be sure of one thing—your past employees and your past customers got it.

METAPHOR FOR CULTURE: THE ATOM AND THE ORGANIZATION

What does physics, specifically the atom, have to teach us about organizations? Well, as it turns out—a lot.

Atoms are elegant things. They are composed of readily recognizable components: electrons, protons, and sometimes neutrons. The protons and neutrons (bound together by a strong nuclear force) form the nucleus. The electrons and nucleus are bound together by electromagnetic force.

Here's the point. We've all heard of electrons, protons, and neutrons. But we probably don't remember the role electromagnetic force plays in holding the atom together. And when we refer to the strong nuclear force—well, let's be honest—your eyes are probably rolling back into your head. Why? It's really not that interesting.

Organizations are composed of an executive team (which in many organizations clearly needs to be held together by a strong nuclear force) and nonexecutives working at various levels. Holding it all together is an invisible, often unstated, organizational electromagnetic force. We can refer to this as the culture. Culture—the way things get done around here.

But it's the people who actually get work done—people at different levels working in sync with each other and with the executive team to get the work done and establish a positive organizational culture.

In organizations, we celebrate the superstars. We recognize the high performers. Yet, what do we do with the employees who just hold things together—the employees who work silently and out of the limelight? They are often the unsung heroes. They hold things together; they ensure that the organizational electromagnetic force is of sufficient strength.

To be honest, we don't do much with them. In fact, we often don't even notice them until they're gone. Then the structure begins to deteriorate. We hear statements like, "Things don't seem to work quite as smoothly as they once did—I wonder what's wrong?"

Improving organizational performance requires looking into all aspects of employee performance from the visible to the invisible. We often make the mistake of recognizing and considering only the highly visible employees for promotion. We caution you not to fall into this trap. The highly visible employees are not necessarily the best-performing employees, and they are not necessarily the ones making sure that the work gets done—they are just highly visible.

Just like the atom, a stable organization has an executive team, nonexecutive employees, a strong nuclear force, and an organizational electromagnetic force. Ignore the forces that hold the components together, and the result is an unstable organization, which may just deteriorate faster than you can control it.

THE UNSUNG HERO

We would like to spend a moment talking about the "unsung hero" in your organization. That person who "holds things together": the facilitator, the peacemaker, the strategist. Shuttle diplomacy is a good way to describe his or her working style.

This person is well-known by the informal ("shadow") organization and is often the "go-to" person when something needs to get done. Great leaders understand the importance of having these people in the organization. Marginal leaders fail to recognize the critical role these people serve, and hence fail to encourage and reward this behavior.

How do you recognize these people?

- They have tenure in the organization.
- They are often in a managerial or even an executive role.
- They are the people others go to when they need something done.
- They are good boundary spanners (i.e., they impact more than just the area they are responsible for).
- Work they've been associated with is successful and done with minimal fanfare.
- They have institutional memory and use it as a learning and teaching tool to avoid mistakes.

And they are invisible among the political noise, posturing, and positioning that runs rampant in far too many organizations.

In our work in transition management and business growth, one of the first steps we take is to find these people because they are the key to a successful initiative. Don't make the mistake of overlooking or ignoring the people who make things work in your organization. Seek them out; talk to them; encourage them; find ways to reward them. And most of all, find ways to retain them.

ARE YOU SUPPORTING THE "SHADOW" ORGANIZATION?

Wouldn't it be nice if your employees always did what you asked them to do, when you asked them to do it, and for it to have the effect you told them it would have? Actually, it wouldn't be nice at all. What's unfortunate, however, is that there are leaders in organizations who truly believe this is possible or should be the way it's done—and it's a worthy goal to pursue. It's not; it's a fool's quest. And even if you did get this to happen (to get your employees to be absolutely compliant), you would be very disappointed. Why? Because the worst possible thing your employees can do is to do exactly what you ask them to do.

Okay, hold on. Before you get caught up in managerial self-righteousness, think about it. You have employees who are customer facing, you have salespeople who interact with clients and prospects every day; you have back office people. You have a team of employees whose job it is to make the organization successful. And yet somehow you think you know more than they do. Interesting.

So let's examine what happens. You walk into a work area, find what you believe is inefficiency, tell the employees to stop wasting their time, and then you proceed to tell them exactly what they should be spending their time on—then you leave. Or in an executive team meeting, you express dissatisfaction with organizational performance, and you proceed to tell each executive what he or she should be doing to improve his or her areas, adjourn the meeting, and then you leave (another true story).

What have you accomplished? The best answer would be "nothing," but unfortunately, that is probably not what happened. What you have done is activate the network of the shadow organization and initiate a new whispering campaign that spreads your outburst throughout the organization, and not in a complimentary way. It works faster than e-mail (employees can text, tweet, instant message, or worst of all, use social media channels).

When we talk with executives about this, a phrase we often hear is, "I don't have time to waste explaining the obvious." Obvious to whom? Certainly not to your staff. Change by fiat rarely works, and the time you save by telling employees what to do you lose in productivity as they complain to one another about you and why it can't be done. Bright, competent, and talented employees do not take input based on the absence of facts well. Sure, it takes time to change, but change that the employees can understand and buy into on the front end is meaningful change that will make the organization better. When you spend time on organizational improvement—spend it on the front end.

The "shadow" organization exists in all companies, and on its own it is neither good nor bad. You, as the leader—by your behavior and actions—decide which direction it will take. If unattended to by the management, it tends to run as a negative and competing force for employee attention and can even affect performance.

So the first point we want to make is for you to be aware that a "shadow" organization exists. You cannot wish it away nor ignore it into what you hope would be oblivion. It doesn't work that way.

While it's most often referred to in a negative sense, the "shadow" organization can also be used as a powerful force for positive change in an organization.

Here are five actions you can take to engage it and use it in a positive fashion:

1. Identify the informal leaders in the organization. (You know who they are because other employees either gravitate to them or steer clear of them.)
2. Find a relevant way to engage with them informally and regularly (management can facilitate this by "walking around") to better understand the organizational dynamics.
3. Observe vigilantly, and listen actively.
4. Do not react or overreact to what you believe is bad news or information you do not agree with. It is at least

one person's perception or interest, and your reaction speaks louder than your words, particularly when you're being watched for how you will handle the tough stuff.

5. Take the suggestions you hear, and if you can do something about them—do it. If not, explain why so people understand. (We find that many times, employees really don't understand the reasons behind management's decisions and make up their own negative assumptions, starting with why you don't really care about them.)

Some may argue that you are giving up control to this "shadow" organization and its leaders. You are not. You are listening to employee concerns and addressing them openly—both what you can do about them and what you can't. And what you can do is to help your employees better understand the direction of the company. For example, employees may be worried about slow sales and feel you should be considering a different approach. And you actually do have a different approach that's beginning to show results, but you have not yet shared it with your employees.

As a leader, you have opportunities every day to listen and act on good information and good advice. And you also have opportunities to quickly correct misperceptions. Use these opportunities swiftly and sincerely; it will help build a better organization.

AVERT COMPLACENCY

No one will admit he or she is complacent. Employees will tell you they are action-oriented, go-getters, and people who can get things done. Sure, there are people who are exactly like this—the very embodiment of the words we just used. But interestingly, few of them actually describe themselves that way, at least in our experience. They just, well, get things done.

Complacency can be easily seen in organizations. They are the organizations that do the following:

- brand themselves as service-oriented, yet score poorly on customer satisfaction
- hold a plethora of meetings where there is a demand for action, yet not much gets done
- value organizational political skills over competent performance when addressing staff promotions
- start many projects, but complete few
- have more action items coming out of a strategy meeting than a staff twice the size could complete in a decade
- talk a very good game but come up short on measureable performance

They are the organizations that give the impression of action. There's an old adage that says it well: "Big hat, no cattle."

While few of us can have a meaningful impact on these sclerotic organizations, you can definitely have a meaningful impact on your business. As an independent "solopreneur" or as a "partnerprenuer," you are the culture! How you behave, how you act, and how you respond make up the culture of your work and represent the company. So how are you doing? Are you getting things done—or talking about them? Are you making the calls—or planning to make the calls? Are you clear on your personal mission, vision, and values—or do you think that is only for big companies?

People we talk with are often surprised when we ask them about their culture. They respond by reminding us that they are solo practitioners or a small partnership, and how on earth can they have a culture? They remind us that culture is that "soft stuff" that big companies have. Big companies certainly do have a culture—in fact, all companies/organizations have a culture, regardless of their size. And that includes one-person organizations.

To better understand how culture relates to you as a solo or partnerpreneur and why it's important, take a moment to answer these questions:

- What's your mission or the purpose of your business?
- What's your vision?

- What are your values that drive your decisions and behavior on a day-to-day basis?
- Is your purpose in alignment with your passion and capabilities?
- Do you practice what you say? Do you deliver on your word and brand promise?
- And, if we asked your customers, would they concur with your answers?

If you don't know, or if you haven't thought about it, we suggest that you take time to candidly reflect on these questions. The most serious organizations even get outside help with a climate or culture assessment. While you may or may not be pleased with all of the answers, at least you will know where to focus for improvement, as ultimately we find that culture is a magnet or a deterrent for both staff and customers.

HEALTHY CONFLICT

Many people fret about conflict, and some even work actively to avoid it. While contrary to what many of us learned as youngsters ("don't fight," "don't talk back," "don't cause problems"), conflict is normal, and conflict is healthy. In fact, unless there is healthy conflict in your organization and in your business relationships, you are missing business growth opportunities and "leaving money on the table."

Conflict is a misunderstood concept. People still believe conflict is destructive, can harm relationships, and can cause schisms in the organization. They further believe that harmony in executive and management meetings is a sign of team alignment. It is not. It is impossible for talented executives and managers to not have strong opinions and to not have different perspectives on market and organizational conditions and how to address them. If they don't have strong opinions, they do not belong at the table. If they don't express their strong opinions, they are not leaders. And no organization can function effectively with executives and managers who do not have strong opinions or the will to express them.

It is the "manner" in which conflict is expressed and addressed that will make it destructive or additive.

In the absence of healthy conflict,

- bad ideas are unchallenged;
- silence is interpreted as agreement ("artificial harmony");
- team members develop different perspectives and ideas about the future of the business—and don't share them with their colleagues. Personal agendas start and drive from this point;
- performance problems are overlooked or not discussed so as not to challenge, offend, or step on toes;
- employees lose confidence because they are unsure of the direction of the company and question whether their management really cares about them, as likely their ideas and concerns will not be heard and, hence, not addressed.

Overstated? No.

Competing and growing is challenging for many companies. There is no need to further hamper organizational development by not encouraging and expecting open, honest, respectful, vibrant—and healthy—conflict.

Remember, however, not all people are comfortable with conflict. As the leader, it is your responsibility to understand this and work with your employees to demonstrate the value to them, the team, and the organization that comes from sharing their opinions and disagreements openly, honestly, and constructively.

Here, we offer five suggestions to help you build a culture that values and gains from engaging in healthy conflict:

1. Change your paradigm of conflict from wrong, bad, harmful, or a "mess" to a means to demonstrate the value of your people, promote diversity of ideas, and garner improved solutions.

2. Communicate the above message as part of your organizational values.
3. Frame expectations to promote healthy conflict by "playing fair" through establishing guidelines for dealing with conflict:
   a. We expect everyone to contribute ideas and concerns, not only in private, but also in meetings.
   b. We treat each other with respect and courtesy, regardless of disagreement and differences of opinion, while we explore the best answer for our targeted outcome (meaning, minimal interruptions, no putdowns, and looking for solutions versus blaming or whining about the problem).
   c. We hold each other accountable for and in conflict (meaning, we each will contribute, and if one of us isn't, we will encourage and inquire; we will remind one another if we are not "playing nice" by providing "gentle reminders," not put-downs; or by refocusing on the ideal outcome and the best idea—not whose idea—will get us there).
4. Demonstrate it by dealing appropriately with conflict as a norm for conduct and the way you do business.
5. Reinforce it. Invite alternative thinking and opposing ideas to expand ways of finding the best solution. Reward individuals and the team through meaningful, sincere, and specific praise and recognition for engaging in and using conflict to your/the organization's advancement.

DRIVING INNOVATION

Innovation – a key topic of interest today and a magnet attribute for individuals and organizations. The problem, unfortunately, is there's more talk than action.

Andy Stefanovick, in his book *Look at More*[2] (Jossey-Bass, 2011), provides us with an unusual approach on how to instill innovation in your organization:

1. *Encourage provocation.* Incite a heightened state of arousal through purposeful disruptions that cause a change in awareness and mood. (Remember that fear is a barrier to creativity, and stress will deplete it.)
2. *Change your mind-set by insuring.* Solicit and understand other perspectives outside of your own. Interestingly, Stefanovick advises that risk, passion, and "confusion tolerance" are key components or disciplines, if you will, for the right mind-set.
3. *Mechanisms.* Build a context to create and apply innovation. This entails using a specific problem scenario or scenarios to employ innovation.
4. *Measurement.* Identify and use measurable criteria to gauge your use and success of innovation/innovative approaches.
5. *Create momentum.* Allow your employees white space! Don't hover, smother, or drive your staff into the ground. Recharge time and breathing space as a practice are critical for innovation.

We see some of the most successful organizations embedding innovation as a way of doing business, which differentiates them. Are you?

If you want to grow your business and especially if you want to be remarkable—you need to innovate. Otherwise you will float, rudderless, in the sea of sameness.

Many business owners we talk with misunderstand the idea of innovation. They think they have to come up with something big and new: a new product, a new service, a brand-new something. Well, fortunately, innovation doesn't require new. It requires better. It requires meaningfully different. In etymology, the word *innovation* derives from the Latin word *innovates,* which is the noun form of *innovare, meaning* "to renew or change." We believe this is an important clarification regarding the common confusion between innovation and creation/invention.

Simply put, innovation can be

- a better approach to customer service;
- a faster response time;
- a way to have fewer errors;
- more efficient processes that reduce cost without impacting service quality—and may even increase service quality;
- a branding approach that resonates with potential buyers; or
- having a person answer the phone!

If you sell insurance, for example, why should someone do business with you and not another agent? If you sell a training program, why should the client choose you? What makes you special? What makes you stand out? What draws clients to you? What represents more value to them than what your competitors provide?

Remember that when you innovate, you will end up doing something different. It may be a small recalibration that will pay great dividends—something better in the mind of the customer, but different from the way you've done business in the past.

Innovation is the ability to change and transform your business practices within your company. To innovate successfully, you must embrace the two sides of innovation: the customer-facing side and the employee-delivery side. Leave one out, and all you have is an unsuccessful project.

TRIBALISM

It's not a word we hear very often when referring to behavior within organizations. Yet it is instantly recognizable, bringing to mind cliques, unions, professional associations, and special-interest groups.

The idea of organizational tribes is neutral. Seth Godin in his book *Tribes*[3] (Penguin Group, 2008) discussed the various kinds of tribes that form around topics of mutual interest among like-minded people. He argued the case that tribes provide leadership opportunities.

Tribes can also cause organizational harm and disruption by

- reducing communication;
- reducing cooperation;
- reducing teamwork (except within the tribe);
- creating self-protective boundaries.

If you are a member of the tribe, you have certain behaviors that are required of you to remain a member; you must conform. If you don't, you're ostracized. And what takes precedence—the good of the organization (i.e., customesr, clients, patients, or students) or the good of the tribe? It's often the good of the tribe to the detriment of the organization's constituency. We often see this in health care, education, and unionized workplaces.

Education is under scrutiny because of poor student scores and progress. Health care is under scrutiny because of poor quality and high cost. Some manufacturing plants are no longer competitive due to union-negotiated wages and benefits.

The protectionism and isolationism that tribes help create is no longer a viable strategy: not in education, not in health care, and not in business. And, yes, we do know the reason for the existence of tribes and why they were important in the past. But times have changed; today we are working in and competing in an international marketplace.

Now the "so what" factor—why does it matter? It matters because to compete, to provide good education, to provide good health care, the organization must perform. It simply cannot perform if people and groups of people are working at cross-purposes (i.e., doctors and administrators; teachers and school administration).

It is naïve to think that cliques will disappear, unions will fade away, or professions will give up their identities. It will not happen. What can happen, however, is what happened in the early 1600s among the Iroquois Indians—they formed a federation, a cooperative to ensure that each tribe not only survived, but thrived. We have historical precedents. The question is—can we learn from them in the twenty-first century?

In whatever form tribalism shows up, if left unattended or ignored, it can be an insidious drain on the organization, its people, and its resources.

Let's focus for a moment on the silo grouping that can manifest tribalism—"mine versus ours." While easy to recognize, it's a challenge to deal with because it is a result of management's decisions. In an attempt to improve organizational performance, organizations often restructure, and very often the law of unintended consequences takes over. (By that we mean that the expected result does not happen, and performance actually gets worse. Like a chronic disease, such behavior is debilitating to the organization and causes disease with the employees. And, actually, chronic reorganization is one sign of a failing company.)

Here are five tips for executives to mitigate tribalism created by silos:

1. Understand your market, the company's competitive position in the market, and what can be done to improve competitive performance to best position your company. (Many leaders miss this first step and jump to number two. This step is critical to align your company to market opportunity—which should relate to your mission and vision and serve to align your people.)
2. Understand what is or is not working now in the company (in its current state), and why.
   a. Is it people, processes, technology, or some other contributor?
3. Design an organizational structure that best addresses the market and organizational performance issues identified above.
4. Identify candidates for leadership positions within the new structure by looking at their performance profile, including their
   a. ability to work in and with teams;
   b. ability to share credit and recognition;
   c. ability to adjust to changing situations.

5. Design meaningful and effective compensation and incentive systems that reward working cooperatively and collaboratively.

THE VALUE OF VALUES ALIGNMENT

What benefits does an organization gain by having values alignment? And what outcomes can be expected if accomplished?

Values, and the alignment of those values across the organization, drive organizational performance and promote growth.

Organizational values reveal themselves in two ways:

1. From organizational strategy development (the planning process to set goals and vision—the ideal future state you are working toward)
2. Through organizational norms that reveal themselves based on behavior (good or bad) in lieu of, or in addition to, established and known values, as set in number one.

Values (also referred to as guiding principles) are one of the three key strategic visionary elements that establish a business philosophy and set the framework for accomplishing work. The other two are vision (where we are going, what our ideal scene is) and mission or purpose (what we do, why we exist).

Generally, executives (the leadership team) set the framework, and staff executes it. If the values are not known, poorly understood, or not supported (i.e., given "lip service"), the benefits of the values run amok. And, as in the case of number two, if values are not identified and shared, they will be made up and driven by the strongest personalities (both positive and negative), often creating dissonance or, worse, a negative culture. As long as this is either tolerated or supported (through inattention), organizational progress will be limited.

The benefits of value alignment are both tangible and intangible. For example, we see three common and potent areas of benefits:

1. Increased quality, productivity, efficiency, and/or effectiveness—tangible elements such as product quality, timing, and satisfaction, which are surfaced through values
   like "excellence," the "gold standard," or "market leaders"
   in services and products;
2. Greater morale and cooperation, which are intangibles
   and derived from values like "respect," "teamwork,"
   "trust," "care," etc., that all work to ultimately promote
   better performance;
3. Increased employee engagement, which is tangible and
   observed in a person's direct work output and activities
   and reflective of values like "accountability," "growth,"
   "individual contribution," "ownership," etc. This also
   crosses into the intangible of positive employee experience at work and is an enabler for morale.

Conversely, a lack of awareness and alignment of the
organizational values will result in employee disengagement,
competition versus cooperation, more insular work and
territoriality versus resource sharing, a decrease in morale,
and ultimately a decrease in productivity—all costly behaviors
that can be avoided. Simply stated, lack of values and
organizational alignment can diminish performance and
impede growth. Often the executive team has no idea why the
organization isn't more successful and argues it can't possibly
be this "values" fluff.

Organizational values are a foundational element of high-
performing organizations. They establish what is most important to getting work done in an organization. They also serve
as a guide to decision-making by enabling staff to assess fit
and priority of business activities and opportunities, which
in turn results in the performance organizational leaders are
seeking.

THE HAPPINESS LINK TO BETTER PERFORMANCE

The link between happiness and better performance gives employers a strong reason to create a positive work environment that is responsive to the needs and interests of their employees.

Research around employee well-being and happiness shows a convincing correlation to heightened productivity, sales, and creativity when employees are happier. And sustained employee performance results in a growing organization.

What should you/the employer pay attention to?

At the core, it's important to create a positive work environment built on the values of supportive relationships, civility, and an experience of learning and growth. Growth comes when the people who have to make it happen are aligned. Internal competition and contention create and then reinforce silos.

While it seems obvious that a happy employee makes a better employee, many employers underestimate or overlook their opportunity to improve business through focusing on their employee's experience (which directly influences happiness). And small consistent experiences of happiness (i.e., positive colleague relationships and supervisory support and feedback) positively move the needle toward a more steady state of happiness.

Additionally, we believe the most progressive employers

- build in creative outlets for employees, such as music, art, or quiet reflection areas or nap rooms;
- offer health and wellness programs through physical exercise opportunities on site and/or work time approved for health and exercise activities;
- promote internal appreciation and expression of gratitude through values and practices;
- support employee contributions to altruistic causes.

Not sure? Think this is fluff and not relevant to the hardcore, hard-driving business world you live in? Well take a look at Google, Zappos, and the work coming out of the Ross School of Business's Center for Positive Organizational Scholarship (University of Michigan). The link between employee happiness and performance is more than an assumption, and it is mutually beneficial to both the employee and the organization.

What's your next step in promoting your employees' happiness?

CULTURE AND EMPLOYEE EMOTIONAL EQUITY

The best companies have executives who actively attend to their organizational culture.

Unfortunately, we find that this is often overlooked and seen as less important than the hard business functions. What's important to understand is that culture is the fluid that keeps the organization's engine running. We preach and prove that culture not only attracts, but, more importantly, helps you keep top talent. And culture—"the way work gets done around here"—as demonstrated by your employees' day-to-day beliefs, attitudes, and behaviors—enables sustainable delivery of your brand promise.

Let's explore the idea of emotional capital or equity. External emotional capital has been described as the value of the feelings and perceptions held by the customer and the external stake-holder toward your business. Emotional equity of your employees is their emotional connection to the company. And in its highest form, it shows up as a deep sense of commitment and loyalty.

Executives who actively work on their culture, in essence, are working to increase their employees' emotional equity. When we help leaders with culture building, we help them address three key elements:

1. Embedding common understanding of and living their values—that is, core values or guiding principles regarding what's most important in how you work together and serve your customers
2. A clear mission and vision statement that articulates what it is that you do, and what it is that the company and its members are ideally working to achieve
3. A strong people plan that identifies your next generation of leaders (a succession management program) and lends for career growth and development for all employees. This often includes the following:
   a. a standardized, meaningful performance appraisal system—remember more regular, informal performance conversations trump the annual review
   b. growth pathways or career ladders for each position, which include options for content experts or management tracks
   c. individual development plans
   d. leadership development program
   e. periodic training
   f. coaching for key executives and new managers

So, when you really understand that your talent is your key resource for delivery and that you can clearly influence your employees' experience in and loyalty to your company; the investment becomes a must versus a wish. And it will pay off.

MANAGING THE GAP BETWEEN YOUR ACTUAL CULTURE AND YOUR INTENDED CULTURE

Your organization has an "experienced reality" by your employees. Do you know what it is? And, do you know how it compares to your stated organizational values?

Values are the underpinning of an organization's culture. A lack of articulated values results in a Wild West culture. And stated but not lived values represent the gap between what you say your values are (you know—the platitudes hanging on the walls) and actual behaviors of the employees within the organization. And this gap results in a lack of trust in leadership, competing interests within the organization, misaligned efforts of your employees and divisions, and in the worst cases of unattended culture—development of a shadow sub-organization.

There are three key takeaways for business leaders to consider from the above:

1. Core values are foundational to your culture—they must be identified, defined in behavioral terms, articulated (communicated across the organization), practiced and then integrated across your Talent Management or People Plan and continuously reinforced during
   a. recruiting;
   b. onboarding;
   c. performance appraisals.
4. Once successfully embedded into your organization, it's important to keep your finger on the pulse in order to assess and close the gap (if necessary) between current employee perceptions and realities and the intended culture. This requires an ongoing assessment of your culture. We recommend an annual survey—especially if
   a. yours is a fast-growth company—whether through organic growth or through acquisitions);
   b. you initiated a change initiative (change can cause cultural disruption).
3. Culture is critical because it defines the day-to-day experience of your employees in your company. And one thing is certain: employees will share their experience about you and your organization with others, and, ultimately, this shapes your brand.

PART FOUR

<hr>

PROGRESSIVE TALENT MANAGEMENT

CHAPTER

7

PROGRESSIVE TALENT MANAGEMENT

This chapter is devoted solely to talent: bringing new talent into your organization and growing and developing these employees for their best contribution to your business.

Up to this point, we have described the parallel benefits of the gravitational organization: customer attraction and retention and talent attraction and retention. A gravitational organization, however, requires attracting and retaining talent in order to attract and retain customers.

Common symptoms of poor talent management include the following:

- low employee engagement
- high turnover
- nonexistent or unwieldy HR processes
- nonexistent or low (emerging) leadership pipeline
- compensation not in alignment with the market
- difficulty hiring

Organizations struggle with talent management for several reasons: foremost, is a lack of management priority and buy-in. Second, the complexity of the implementation-based, integrative nature of talent management and costs in time and resources quickly follow as a key challenge in talent management.

Talent management is the fourth element in the gravitational organization triangle. It's the process of attracting, selecting, developing, and promoting employees through the organization.

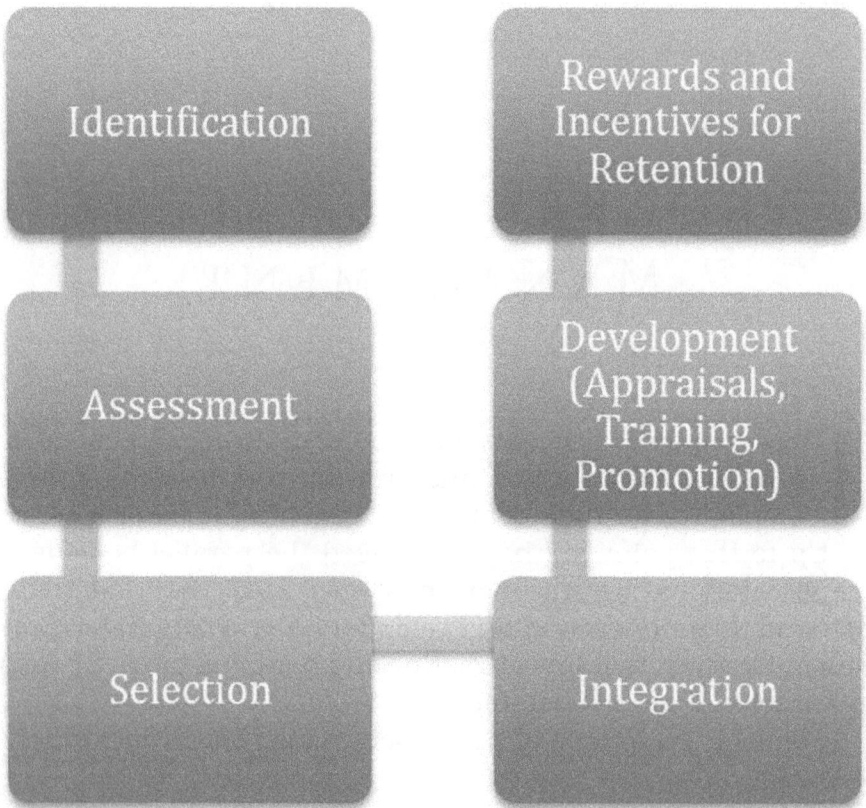

Identification	Rewards and Incentives for Retention
Assessment	Development (Appraisals, Training, Promotion)
Selection	Integration

If you believe that talent development and management starts with selection, you are not alone, but you are incorrect. Many business owners and executives think about the talent process the same way. And this is part of the concern we have regarding the talent process.

IDENTIFICATION — TARGETING THE TALENT YOU NEED

Great talent does not just show up at your door. The idea behind becoming a gravitational organization is to take positive steps (through branding and culture) to attract the prospective candidate's attention. This requires a plan.

When you create a brand strategy, you define the market you want to focus on and address the issues you believe your prospects have that your product or service can address. In other words, you target your market.

It's the same with talent. You target where you want to get your brand and culture message out. It may be college-recruiting initiatives, developing close working relationships with select professors and colleges, job fairs, or key industry events and associations. It can be a variety of outreach programs. Simply put—in today's talent shortage market—you need to get the word out.

If you are a Google, Apple, or Microsoft, candidates come to you. If you are a small or medium-size business (SMB) some candidates may come to you, but most will need a nudge. They will need to be aware of and learn about you, and for them to learn about you, you need to "get out there."

Now, does this mean that the ideas we shared for brand and culture don't really work for attracting candidates? Not at all; candidates need to learn about you, and where are they likely to go after they've heard about you? Right—to the Internet, predominantly your website and social media. And what do they say about you? In other words, what is your brand and how are you known for keeping your promise (culture)? Yes, it's an interlacing web of strategies, but that's what the business market is today.

A very basic issue is your website. Every knowledgeable (and not-so-knowledgeable) candidate will visit your website before he or she visits you. What is the impression he or she is left with? What experience does your "Career" or "Join" section on your website provide? This matters for today's workforce, and it matters a lot.

ASSESSMENT — THE PRECURSOR TO THE RIGHT SELECTION

Whether you have more candidates than you have positions or only one candidate for the job, talent assessment is important. Having a "warm body" in place just doesn't cut it. It doesn't cut it because the "warm body" may be qualified on paper, but also may be an interpersonal train wreck that will eat into your culture faster than a beaver shreds a tree. You do not need dams built in your company. (Note: Dams are also referred to as bottlenecks in process improvement parlance, and bottlenecks prevent work from getting done efficiently and effectively, thus contributing to a negative hold in your culture.)

There are seven steps to consider that we believe are critical, yet often overlooked in the initial (new candidate) talent assessment phase:

1. Make sure the hiring manager (you or one of your subordinates) has accurately assessed
   a. what the job requires;
   b. what needs to be done (versus what is stated on an outdated job description—if you have one);
   c. what skills, behaviors, and attitudes are required to achieve the requirements for success;
   d. what role adaptation is anticipated for the future.
2. Consider initial small-group interviews, where candidates are asked questions respective to their aspirations, career motivators, and interests. This can help determine leadership qualities and cultural fit, as well as interpersonal dynamics.

3. Use behaviorally based interview questions that probe the candidate's experience history, decisions made, and results achieved.

4. Include specific culture-based questions to help determine the candidate's values and compare them to your organizational values. A key query to use is, "Tell me about your ideal company culture." (Ask before you talk about your own company's culture.)

5. Include a scenario-based problem for the candidate to resolve and report on.

6. Share with the candidate your organization's talent integration process along with comments and stories from staff who have experienced its value.

7. Consider having top candidates complete a personality-based job performance indicator/assessment that measures their potential for success in different business environments and roles. (Though such an assessment should never be used as the sole criterion for selection, as part of a selection set, it can be a valuable tool to avoid hiring the wrong candidate for the job.) This assessment can also be used as a tool to support and coach the new employee in areas that need to be addressed to promote a faster and more effective integration.

SELECTION — GETTING THE RIGHT PEOPLE FOR THE JOB AND YOUR ORGANIZATION

You are now at a point where you can select. You may be selecting from a pool of one, but if you followed the path described above, you will at least be assured that you have done your due diligence.

Regardless of how badly you need an employee, a bad or marginal employee is *never* a good decision. Sure, your growth may be hampered until you find a suitable candidate, but a poor candidate can result in not just hampering growth, but decreasing growth due to his or her toxic effect on the company and possibly your customers and clients as well. In this scenario, no choice is much better than a bad choice.

If you have multiple candidates, evaluate each candidate on a "musts" versus "wants" scale. Here, we are suggesting that you dispassionately address what the successful candidate *must* bring to the job to be successful. Oftentimes we see employers saying the following:

- We need someone who has a master's degree.
- We need someone with ten years of experience.
- We need someone who has not changed jobs too often, or who has not stayed in one place for too long.
- We need someone who has done the exact work we need done.

While these objectives are admirable, how many are truly required (versus desired) for the candidate to be a success?

- Do you need someone with a master's degree, or do you need a content expert?
- Do you need someone with ten years of experience, or will five great years do?
- Do you know why the person changed jobs or didn't, and how do the actual reasons fit with your hiring needs?
- The chance of finding a candidate who has done the exact same work you need done severely limits your candidate pool and assumes that bringing different skills and experiences to the workplace has no value.

Think about a *must* list that looks something like this one:

- The candidate must have had different job experiences.
- The candidate must have skills and behaviors different from our current employees.

- The candidate must have interests and activities outside of his or her work.
- The candidate must have demonstrated learning agility and progressive growth and advancement in his or her experience and roles.

Now, we are not saying that our list of *musts* should apply to you. What we are encouraging is approaching candidate selection with an open mind and with a focus on how the candidate can grow and develop into a bigger role (if that is an interest for him or her) as your company grows. Why? Because in a fast-growing company, you are really hiring for future needs, and the current role is just transitional.

Don't limit yourself. What we find more important than a list of job "specs" is a clear understanding of what attributes, experience, and knowledge the candidate needs to possess in order to accomplish the identified key responsibilities and outcomes of the job successfully in the next year or two, with the ability to adapt, grow, and evolve with the company.

INTEGRATION — SWIFT INCLUSION

We define talent integration as the process and practice of blending (integrating) new hires into the organization. A second level of talent integration includes the process and practice for integrating newly promoted managers and executives into their new roles.

Too often, this process is overlooked in SMBs or simplified in larger organizations through a quick orientation or onboarding process. This leaves people to fend for themselves and attempt to adjust to their new organization and roles essentially on their own. This practice negatively influences their productivity and personal experience. It will also lower the perception your new employee has about your company, and ultimately your top talent will leave. They will leave because they have options. Employees want to feel important, and they want to feel that they have been given a good opportunity to integrate into their new organization.

We mentioned earlier the problems with a quick orientation or onboarding process. Let's explain, as challenging the onboarding process may appear on the surface to be an odd approach. Onboarding, by definition, is intended to help new employees acquire the necessary knowledge, skills, and behaviors to become effective members of the organization. Onboarding tactics that companies commonly use include formal meetings, lectures, videos, print materials, or computer-based orientations. Yet, what we see is that these processes often default to a more mechanical and routine approach (checklist-style) than to a true process of personal and social (and cultural) integration with a developmental approach.

The key purpose of talent integration is to reduce the time for those new hires in becoming productive contributors (i.e., shorten the new job learning curve) and to anchor them swiftly into the organization through establishing strong relationships, support, and loyalty. This practice helps them be successful corporate citizens sooner and helps retain employees. Strong "enculturation" also serves as a differentiator and becomes another way to attract talent to your organization.

Talent integration involves a more formal, developmentally focused transition plan to help the new employee integrate into your organization—usually covering at least the first 90 to 180 days on the job (positions with greater responsibility for company strategy and positions that require a skills transition, such as clinical/technical employees who are promoted to managers, require additional transition time). In addition to the standard onboarding tactics named above, it includes four core elements:

1. A foundational discussion between the new staff and his or her immediate supervisor within the first days of hire to
   a. define clear expectations regarding job performance and key expected results to focus on in the next year;

    b. discuss how best to work with each other. Consider requirements and individual preferences for communication frequency and methods.

2. Internal mentorship to foster relationship building for the new employee to help him or her understand the organizational culture and "how work gets done around here"

3. Coaching for new managers (best done with an external/ neutral executive/performance coach) to support the transition, especially if new skills are needed (such as when a technical/clinical person is promoted to a manager). Remember, *What Got You Here Won't Get You There* (Marshal Goldsmith's book by the same name, 2007)

4. Regular performance feedback meetings (focusing on frequent, informal conversations for at least the first 90 to 180 days) focusing on what is going well (and why), where the person is challenged, what his or her ideas are, what he or she could use for help, and how he or she is adapting to the organization. These discussions are dialogues and iterative in nature, versus a monologue from the boss.

DEVELOPMENT — HELPING YOUR EMPLOYEES REACH THEIR FULL POTENTIAL

Your candidate will clearly bring skills to the organization in addition to potential: the potential to learn more, the potential to grow, and the potential to make a significant impact on your organization. But this rarely happens on its own.

We started this book with a physics metaphor using the concept of gravity. Let's stay, for a moment, with physics and discuss the concept of entropy. The dictionary definition of *entropy* is revealing:

- For a closed thermodynamic system, a quantitative measure of thermal energy not available to do work

- A measure of disorder or randomness in a closed system
- A measure of the loss of information in a transmitted message
- The tendency for all matter in the universe to evolve to a state of inert uniformity
- Inevitable and steady deterioration of a system or society

As you read this, think about your employees, who, left to fend for themselves in your company, will demonstrate the human version of entropy in your organization. They will have a tendency to evolve to a state of inert uniformity.

Employees are the predominant asset to your business. You work to have your assets produce positive returns. To achieve a positive return, you need to invest in your assets. Employees are no different.

So what do you do? Just like in physics, you infuse energy (i.e., invest) into the system. Here are some ways to do that:

- Implement a constructive, meaningful, and regular employee appraisal system tied to the values and strategic goals of the company. Conduct semi-annual performance reviews that include self-assessments and collaborative goal-setting that focus on the following:
    o skills learned
    o skills demonstrated
    o skills to be learned
    o what went well
    o what can be done better
    o professional goals
  A practice of regular, informal development check-ins should continue throughout the year. And inherent in a "regular and meaningful appraisal process" is communication and a positive supervisor/employee relationship.
- Create individualized and targeted formal and informal training and educational opportunities to help

employees grow and build upon their strengths and capabilities, such as
   o targeted course work at a college or university
   o advanced degree programs
   o internal "residency" programs
   o seminars and workshops
   o conferences
   o professional association-sponsored programs
   o e-learning
   o management training
   o leadership development.
- Give "stretch" assignments that demonstrate skills and enable the candidate to learn new skills and develop skills that will be required for growth and advancement in your organization.
- Mentor and coach:
   o Mentoring involves having a more experienced, "tenured," and successful employee mentor (or serve as a guide) to the employee.
   o Coaching is more formal, and usually involves an outside coach.

As the leader, you may use only some of these developmental tools. But one tool should be foremost in your mind and an operating "must" in your organization, and that is the performance review. The performance review process, done well and done consistently, is a powerful tool to employee development, engagement, and retention.

REWARDS AND INCENTIVES — MATCHING WHAT MAKES THEM TICK

Investing in top talent only to lose them is not just expensive; it is demoralizing.

Talent retention starts with the actions we noted above:

- good experience during the selection process
- good experience when they start with the company
- good integration experience
- consistent and useful performance appraisals
- opportunities to learn and grow
- opportunity to have a mentor or coach

But this is not enough. You need to follow through and ensure you have an effective <u>incentive and rewards program.</u> Specifically, performance-based incentives and individual and team recognitions are important and under-used components of talent management.

The evidence-based power of employee recognition as tied to employee productivity, engagement, and retention is well addressed in *The Carrot Principle*[1] (Gostick and Elton, 2007; 2009). People's internal motivations trigger differently. Some like accolades; some like rewards; and some want something to strive for—a goal. Some want to get promoted; some want to be the best at what they do, and a promotion will likely encourage them to leave the company. But there is one commonality—no one likes to be taken for granted, ignored, or overlooked. And managers who offer constructive praise and meaningful rewards motivate employees to excel.

The attitude of "okay, we got them; now on to the next one" is organizational suicide. It also speaks loudly and not in a complimentary way about your culture.

A December 2011 article in *Forbes* magazine by Eric Jackson[2] listed the top ten reasons why large companies fail to keep top talent. As you read these, think about your company. Think about the opportunity it presents you not only to recruit talent from large companies, but also as clues to what you need to do to retain them in your company. In our experience, we find the very same issues in SMBs. And don't for a minute believe that SMBs really don't have a bureaucracy. They most certainly do.

Here are the top ten reasons why large companies fail to keep talent:

- big-company bureaucracy
- failure to find a project for the talent that ignites their passion
- poor annual performance reviews
- no discussion around career development
- shifting whims/strategic priorities
- lack of accountability and/or telling them how to do their job
- top talent likes to be with other top talent
- the missing vision thing
- lack of open-mindedness
- lack of leadership (not knowing who is really in charge and makes the decisions)

Talent management is a longitudinal process; it's not an event. You don't hire an employee and just assume he or she will start contributing on day one. That is an incorrect assumption and a contributor to what is often referred to as a "hiring mistake."

Remember our metaphor about entropy. In the physical world, energy needs to be applied to a system to prevent entropy. It's the same with employees—and with organizations, for that matter.

In the changing demographic of the employee population, talent development and management is an important differentiator.

The only way work gets done, the only way strategy becomes reality, the only way new ideas are brought to market, the only way value is added to your product or service, and the only way customers become delighted with you and your service is through your people. Mess this up, and the rest just doesn't matter.

TALENT MANAGEMENT SUPPLEMENT: A SERIES OF TIPS AND TECHNIQUES TO DRIVE PROGRESSIVE TALENT MANAGEMENT

TALENT RECRUITING AND INTEGRATION — FOUR PRIMERS THAT CREATE SUCCESS

If you honestly believe that people are assets to your organization, if you want to maintain a competitive advantage in the marketplace, and if you are serious about managing costs, then talent recruiting and integration is a must for your people strategy.

Talent integration involves working with new managers and executives (whether promoted from within or hired into the company) to transition them quickly and effectively into their new roles. The key purpose of talent integration is to reduce the time for those new to their roles to become productive contributors (i.e., shorten the new-job learning curve).

Talent integration involves these activities:

- A formal transition plan to help the manager/executive integrate into the organization—usually covering the first ninety days.
- A formal and purposeful discussion between the new managers/executives and their immediate supervisors on how best to work with each other and to define clear expectations regarding job performance and expected results. (For more information on this, see the "Transitioning Middle Managers" section later in this chapter.)
- Internal mentorship to help the new manager/executive better understand the organizational culture, the players, and "how work gets done here."
- Coaching (best done with an external/neutral executive/ performance coach)—to help personally with the transition, especially if new skills are needed (i.e., a technical/ clinical person is promoted to a manager).

Clearly, talent integration done well requires frontloading in investment and hiring or promoting the right employee. But recruiting top talent is a challenge for all organizations, and the success rate is disappointing. A good hire not properly integrated into the position and the organization will lead to poor performance of the individual, which in turn often leads to a host of other issues that impact the department or organization, such as retention problems, morale issues, and even customer service or product quality issues. Then, painfully, you find yourself back at the beginning—recruiting, which can and does become a vicious and expensive cycle. We see it more than we would like. The great news is that is it correctable.

While recruiting is an explicit cost, the more significant cost of not having a talent integration process is the opportunity cost created by a lack of focus and concentration on the work and the marketplace. But it starts with recruiting—or promoting—the right person to address the needs of the organization.

INTELLIGENT SELECTION LEADS TALENT INTEGRATION

In the 1989 movie *Field of Dreams*, Ray Kinsella (played by Kevin Costner) hears a voice as he walks through his cornfield: "If you build it, he will come." Over the years, this saying has since become part of our lexicon of misused quotes and has morphed into phrases like, "If you build it, they will come."

We see this kind of thinking seep into talent integration—if you hire them (or promote them), they will contribute. Well, to use another well-known phrase—not exactly. Why would we honestly believe that hiring or promoting a person into a new job will result in immediate success? The hiring retention success rate is dismal; some studies report a rate lower than 50 percent. Without knowing the job requirements, what needs to be done, and what skills, behaviors, and attitudes are required for success, you might as well spend your money on a trip to Las Vegas to roll the dice. The chance of winning is about the same—or maybe slightly better in Vegas, and you will likely have more fun.

The standard ingredients for selecting candidates are the following:

- an application and/or résumé
- the interview
- references

However, these all tell you only what the candidate wants you to know. (Read: Good creative writing and strong impression management skills do not necessarily equal the most suitable candidate.) Have you ever hired someone who appeared to be perfect for the job, only to find out later that he or she did not have the ability to do the job? Costly mistake? Exactly! So let's dig deeper.

Just because someone can report experience on a résumé does not mean he or she has the personality to do the job. For example, we saw one of our clients hire a department director who was charged with turning around an underperforming department. He appeared to be well-qualified, coming from a department that recently had undergone a very successful turn-around. He was the assistant director. He floundered in the new job. One of the reasons was that he was too empathetic and had a very high interpersonal sensitivity toward others. Simply put, he could not make the tough people decisions. Nowhere on the résumé, during the interview, or in interviews with the hand-picked references did this come out.

To integrate talent well, you need to start with talent integration potential. Just as you cannot fit a square peg into a round hole (without damage), you cannot make a person who does not have the basic ingredients for success successful *in the job* you need done. This does not mean the person cannot be successful; it just means he or she will not likely be successful in a particular job.

How do you know? Consider having your selected candidates take a personality-based, job performance indicator test, which measures a candidate's potential for success in different business environments. Such an assessment should never be used as the sole criterion for selection. But as part of a selection set, it can be an invaluable tool. It can also be used as a tool to coach the new employee in areas that need to be addressed to ensure a fast and effective integration into a new job. We all have derailers (personality traits and risk behaviors that can sabotage our success). When we know them, we can deal with them. The better we deal with them, the better we perform in our new jobs. Everyone wins.

Internal Talent Recruiting and Integration

How does your organization promote from within? Do you select the person who is doing the best job in his or her current role? Do you promote the person you like the most, the person who has the most seniority, or the person who gives you attention and deference? If any of these is your current practice, then you are missing out on the opportunity to grow your business. You may also be dramatically increasing your cost of operations. This is hardly a good strategy.

Let's take a moment to look at the cost of a bad (mismatched) promotion:

- time spent to become productive on the job
- time to separate from being a peer to being a boss
- turnover cost resulting from a bad promotion
- lost productivity resulting from the turnover
- recruiting cost

A poor promotional decision is costly.

Internal promotions should be approached the same way you approach external hires: formally. There are distinct advantages you have when promoting from within. The candidates know the business, know some of the politics (politics at the managerial and executive level, however, are different), and are familiar with the culture. But this knowledge alone should not qualify them for promotion. What qualifies them for promotion is a positive performance track record and demonstrated ability (versus just an interest or a willingness) to take on additional responsibilities to succeed.

There are five actions organizations should take to prepare internal candidates for promotion:

1. Have a formal (or at least an informal) succession plan. Identify individuals within your organization who can fill current senior positions (should the incumbent retire or leave) or new positions that are created due to growth,

new product or service introductions, or new projects critical to the success of the company.

2. Implement a management development program to provide future promotable candidates the opportunity to take on additional and more challenging responsibilities. A management development program will also identify employee strengths, preferences, values, and potential derailers to promote the best fit for positions available.

3. Introduce a valid and meaningful 360-degree evaluation program (i.e., a 360 evaluation program involves feedback from the individuals' boss, subordinates, and peers) to ensure that the candidates identified for promotion are truly qualified and not just good at managing up (i.e., individuals who are very attentive, responsive, and respectful to their bosses, but behave in a very different and negative way to peers and subordinates) and managing their images.

4. Provide the future promotable candidates with a mentor to help guide them through both the tangible and intangible aspects of achieving success within the company.

5. Provide the newly promoted employees with coaching support to support the transition from a functional focus to a manager with broader responsibilities.

Companies should use a mix of internal and external hires to build their teams, with the larger number coming internally. A rigorous internal promotion process will best prepare candidates, strengthen the business, and, ultimately, benefit your customers.

EXTERNAL RECRUITING

Sometimes, however, companies need to recruit external talent. Unfortunately, many companies believe they have found the holy grail of talent when they identify and bring in a manager from outside. Listening to the executive team and hiring managers, you could think you were watching the movie *WarGames*, as you hear those immortal words, "Confidence is high! I repeat, confidence is high!" Far too often—some statistics say up to 50 percent of the time—the candidate crashes and burns. What went wrong? Everything seemed to point to guaranteed success.

In situations like this, we find three things went wrong:

1. Not clearly understanding the job that needed to be done
2. Not clearly understanding the organizational context in which the new manager will work
3. Poor candidate vetting (meaning a mismatch in the skills and attributes of the new manager to the role and/ or the organization itself)

If you do not know the job that needs to be done (which Michael D. Watkins[1] defines as start-up, turnaround, accelerated growth, realignment, or sustaining success), then finding the right candidate for the job is a stochastic event. The best way to determine what job needs to be done is to ask. Understand what needs to be done. This is really a 360-degree review of the department or the operating unit.

Organizations have personalities. They have established cultures, and many can behave like the body's immune system—ravaging foreign invaders that appear to be a threat to the system. We had a client who hired a CIO who did not represent the culture of the organization. He was direct and abrasive. The organizational members were polite. The hiring manager believed the CIO would "shake things up." The only person who got shaken up, though, was the new hire. He lasted six months, even amidst a "polite" culture.

When you know the job that needs to be done, and you have an understanding of the culture of the organization, you can then outline the skills and behaviors that the ideal candidate should possess. As we discussed previously, it is helpful to break down the skills and behaviors into "musts" and "wants"—that is, the non-negotiables versus the would-be-nice-to-haves. No candidate can meet all the criteria an organization can mobilize in the selection process. (As a note—think about the incumbents in a job—do they meet *all* the criteria you are setting out for the new hire? And if you say you want people "better than I" or "better than our current staff" so we can get better as an organization, that's outstanding—if that is really what you mean.) But the successful candidate must at least meet all of the "musts." As mentioned above, we recommend a personality-based assessment and job-performance indicator that measures a candidate's potential for success. We also recommend an interview process that includes superiors, peers, and subordinates. Also, we assume that the job (that is, the current and necessary essential functions of the job) has been assessed and accurately captured on a written job description to frame expectations clearly from the beginning.

Hiring candidates from outside the organization can be a risk for both the candidate and the organization. It is important to make a concerted effort to reduce the risk and increase the chance for success. Not only does everyone win, but more importantly, work gets done, the company continues to grow, and you do not end up with a retention problem.

Talent integration is essential for organizational success. But it starts with a thoughtful and detailed recruiting process, whether the candidate comes from within the organization or from outside the organization. Assuming that a talented person will show up and begin producing great work is naïve and reckless. If you want your organization to grow, if you want to minimize disruptions, if you want to reduce turnover, and if you want to control costs, start with recruiting and integrating the right talent.

HIRING FOR FAST-GROWING DEPARTMENTS OR COMPANIES

To be a fast-growing company—whether a start-up or a new growth unit within a large corporation—there first needs to be a product or service that is priced right, and that customers are interested in and are actively buying. The company also needs to hire and manage people well, and you—as the owner, recruiting executive, or HR manager in charge—are faced with managing rapid growth.

The typical hiring questions that come up are ones like these:

- Who do we hire?
- Where do we find them?
- What should we pay them?
- How do we retain them?

While these questions are important, there are two issues that must be addressed first: alignment and transformability.

Alignment addresses the passion and skills the candidates bring to the organization and their fit within the organization. *Transformability* is hiring the person not for the job as it exists today, but as it will exist tomorrow. Addressing alignment without considering transformability will likely result in hiring the wrong person.

Alignment has three components: passion, skills, and fit. In selecting employees, gauge their passion for the work and for the challenge it represents. Identify the skills needed to support the continuing growth of the company. It could be marketing, sales, operations, or financial skills. Last, evaluate how the person will fit into your organization. Fit, essentially, is how well the person will cope with the "way work is done around here"— the personalities, the pace, and the customers.

Alignment is important, but in isolation of the second component—transformability—it is insufficient to ensure that the right person will be hired. You are not hiring for the job as it exists today; you are hiring for the job as it will likely exist twelve months from today.

Remember, we are talking about a fast-growing company, and one of the characteristics of a fast-growing company is that things change—fast.

Think about the last time you changed jobs. While we all like to believe we hit the ground running, most of us took some time to assimilate into the new job, to the way work gets done, to what is and is not acceptable, and to a myriad of other issues resident in a new organization.

Now consider this: you just start feeling comfortable in your work environment (that is, you have assimilated), and you come to work the next day and the job has changed. Your skills are no longer what is required because what is required now is different. This is a fact of life in fast-growing companies.

So if you are a fast-growing company, when you think about hiring, think about how the job will look twelve months from now. Think about the skills that will be required, and start looking for candidates who fit the future, not just the current, job requirements.

When talking with candidates, tell them what the job is today, how you expect it will change over time, and that you are looking to fill the job as it will likely exist in the future. This way, you are being honest. Some candidates may seriously wonder if you know what you are doing. Others will be energized by the idea that the job will change, and they will not only have a chance to grow, but they will be expected to grow. Fast-changing job requirements are not for the faint of heart. This kind of job ambiguity isn't for everyone, but if you consider alignment and transformability as you start the hiring process, you are being honest with both yourself and with your future employees. The probability that you will hire and retain the right people increases significantly.

Here are nine questions to consider when interviewing for a fast-growing company:

1. Did the candidate show passion for the work and its challenges?
2. Did the candidate demonstrate an ability to tolerate ambiguity?
3. Did the candidate possess general knowledge and skills? Was he or she intelligent?
4. Was the candidate prepared for the interview, and did he or she have interesting ideas about the job, the company, and the product or service?
5. What is the candidate's work history (results) and experience with different roles/jobs?
6. Did the candidate demonstrate an ability to "think on his or her feet"?
7. Is there a cultural fit?
8. Did the candidate present well (read: have a strong positive presence)?
9. Did the candidate challenge you and your thinking during the interview with good questions or another way to look at an issue?

On Hiring

The Perfect Fit Is Rare

How many hours do we waste, how much annoyance do we cause, how much silly time do we tolerate looking for the perfect candidate to fill a vacancy? And it doesn't matter if it's for a CEO position, a department manager, or a front-line worker. We have a revelation for you—the perfect candidate is an anomaly.

Good candidates exist; even excellent candidates exist. But perfect candidates—let alone a pool of them—no. Yet this is where many overspend time in hiring. And what's even more interesting (and frustrating) is when you have a committee doing the selection, in which each person has a different take on what "perfect" is.

Some may argue that a committee with different views of perfection leads to a better choice. Perhaps yes, if the committee has taken the time to align around core functions and the competencies and attributes that will best match prior to interviewing; however, this is unlikely in our experience. So an unaligned, or misaligned, interview committee often leads to infighting, positioning, and a resolution not to work with the new person hired because they don't feel the candidate met their definition of perfect.

Each member of the selection committee defaults to vetting the candidate through his or her lens of what's most important: people from the finance department believe the person needs strong financial acumen; operations people are looking for operational experience; information technology wants strong IT skills, and so on.

And the worst scenario of all is a committee that can only reach a consensus decision. And for these organizations, it's a good thing that finding and hiring a candidate is not a matter of urgency. A quick moment to explain. We are familiar with organizations that state they have a sense of urgency to hire a person, yet drag out the process—sometimes for months.

So when you are first looking to hire, assess, define, and agree upon what you really need for the role. What are the musts and what are the-nice-to-haves? Define these in writing, and then challenge each "must" with why it's a must. Also, understand what business personality you need for the job. Business personality may be categorized as a "soft skill," but it is essential that the candidate's business personality match the work that needs to be done and the culture of the organization.

For example, if you need someone to improve performance and reenergize growth, a laid-back candidate with high interpersonal sensitivity and high empathy is not the candidate you need for the job, regardless of what the résumé may say. Remember, résumés are often an exercise in creative writing, and interviews are really a matter of skill and confidence. So, the real challenge is to use selection methods that will evoke authenticity in the candidate and surface demonstration of his or her skills and attributes as they relate to the position you are hiring for.

How to Decide Who You Need

In our experience, organizations do find outstanding candidates that make significant contributions to the organization. And one interesting factor—sometimes they were not the "perfect candidate" as defined by an all-encompassing job description, but rather a candidate who seemed to have the interest, enthusiasm, willingness to learn and adapt, and general skills to do a good job.

Have you ever seen the following type of write-up as a job description?

> The candidates must have at least ten years of experience in our industry, doing the type of job we are recruiting for. He or she must also be proficient in building teams and have excellent marketing, financial, and people skills. He or she must be able to perform under tight deadlines, understand the legal issues of the work, support diversity, and have significant community involvement. He or she must be willing to travel, including overseas travel. The candidate must also be able to demonstrate work/life balance to the staff. An MBA is required.

Finding the right candidate for your organization requires just two simple yet challenging tasks. These tasks must be completed before the standard or traditional selection process begins:

1. Identify what the job actually requires—what are the key functions and responsibilities?
   a. What's really required to succeed in the job?
   b. Look at who has succeeded and who has not, and determine the difference.

c. Categorize the requirements into musts and wants—
never compromise on a must, and don't get hung up
on a want.

2. Match the requirements with the qualifications, focusing
on the musts.

Once this is done, the interview can focus on how qualified the
candidate is for the job that actually needs to be done (both right
now and considering the growth of the organization and what it
will mean for that role). And the lead decision-maker for the hire
must be the person this candidate will report to.

Finding good candidates is a challenge, but not because you
have to find the perfect candidate. It is a challenge because you
need to find the right candidate for the job. There is a difference,
and successful hiring managers know the difference.

ON TRANSITIONS

WHEN YOU ARE THE NEW HIRE

Being hired from outside the organization has its own set of
challenges. Specifically, you are coming into an organization
that has a set culture, a set way of doing things, and a set value
system and alliances whose purpose is often to maintain the
status quo. Yet, you were hired to improve the organization. How
do you this? You start by thinking through and managing your
transition into the organization.

Michael D. Watkins, in his book *The First 90 Days*[2], offers
the following ten strategies for successfully transitioning into
your new role.

1. Promote yourself. You need to mentally break from your
old job (or company) and accept and extend yourself in
your new role.
2. Accelerate your learning curve. Invest in learning not just
the technical side of your job, but also spend time learning the company's culture and politics.

3. Match strategy to the situation. There is no one strategy that fits all situations. Are you going into a start-up, turnaround, realignment, or sustaining success situation"?

4. Secure early wins. Get started quickly by implementing something that will result in a quick win for you.

5. Negotiate success. It is important to have a good working relationship with your boss, to define expectations, and to discuss how to work together productively.

6. Achieve alignment. It's important to align strategy, structure, systems, skills, and culture and to identify the root cause of problems.

7. Build your team. Assess the current team members based on the job that needs doing, and build your team.

8. Create coalitions. Authority alone will not guarantee success; you need to learn how to influence those from whom you need support.

9. Keep your balance. You need to create and enforce personal discipline and create a network of advisors.

10. Expedite everyone. It's important to accelerate team development, develop high-potential leaders, and strengthen succession planning.

Successfully transitioning into your new role is critical for long-term success. Becoming successful in that role is a transition, and it will take time and thoughtful action. And remember the first strategy on the list—promote yourself. If you fail to, no one else will either.

FIVE IDEAS TO HELP WITH YOUR MOVE TO MANAGEMENT

First, let's be open and honest. You are likely going to feel uncomfortable as you move from the job you knew and did well into a job you don't know as well and may question your ability to do it. This is normal. Based on our experience, we find that many, if not most, new managers feel this way.

Here are five ideas on what you can do to make the transition work for you:

1. Accept the fact that this is a new role, and it will take time and learning to become good at it. Management is not, as some unfortunately believe, easy and something anybody can do. It is a job that requires great skill and a sincere commitment to do well.

2. Find a mentor—someone in the organization that you can talk to. Use him or her to help you navigate the organizational culture and to gauge your effectiveness and test your assumptions about any aspect of the job and the organization.

3. Understand your boss's expectation of you and how he or she would like to work with you. Just because you were promoted by this person doesn't mean he or she is your "friend" and will not hold you to a high performance standard.

4. Promote yourself. You need to see yourself as the manager; you need to assume the role and start behaving and performing as such. If you don't, it is pretty certain that others won't either.

5. Find a coach to help guide you through the transition process. A coach will help you identify the key skills required for your management role, outline what it takes to succeed in the role, and guide you through the initial transition process. Just like rookies on a professional sports team need a coach to help them understand how the game is played at the pro level and guide them through the transition, so do employees new to management.

We recommend that you read *The First 90 Days* by Michael Watkins.

Managers are important to the success of the organization, and it is a role that is certainly worth pursuing and performing well. If you think management is right for you—pursue it aggressively. If, after a solid effort, you truly do not like the role or are not good at it, let it go—for your sake and the sake of your employees.

What Can You Do as a Newly Appointed Manager to Establish Credibility?

A question we frequently get is "How do I deal with my peers who are now my subordinates?" This is an important question. Organizations are a collection of tribes (operating units within the organization—see "Tribalism" in chapter 6). When the social balance is disrupted, as it is with a promotion, instability follows. What can you as the newly appointed manager do to reestablish stability?

We offer six suggestions, which are based on Michael D. Watkins'[3] advice presented in his book, *Your Next Move*:

1. Accept that relationships have to change.
   a. This is a simple reality.

2. Focus early on the rites of passage.
   a. Some of your peers will be pleased, some will be shocked, and some will be angry.
   b. Allow them to go through the grieving cycle—to a point.
   c. If some cannot stop grieving, it is time for them to find a new opportunities.

3. Reenlist your good former employees.
   a. Identify who is important to keep, and be sure to get that message to them.

4. Establish your authority deftly.
   a. Don't oversell your authority, nor undersell it. A middle-of-the-road approach can work the best.

5. Focus on what's good for the business.
   a. You were promoted to advance the business. Make the right decisions with this in mind.

6. Approach team-building with caution.
   a. How you approach team-building starts with knowing the objectives you want to accomplish for the unit and thus the business.

Being promoted is exciting and creates a new career challenge. Approach it thoughtfully and confidently.

Transitioning Middle Managers

The pages of management journals are filled with articles stressing the importance of properly transitioning senior executives into new positions. The ability for these individuals to "hit the ground running" is critical to their integration into the organizational structure and to their ultimate success. These articles are essential, but they often leave out a crucial corollary—the transition of middle managers into their new positions. Middle managers are integral to an organization's ability to perform well. And often they are moving from a skill based role (i.e. clinical, engineering) to a managerial based role. Unfortunately, they often do not always get the attention they deserve to support this transition.

Middle managers play a vital role in the success of an organization by effectively and efficiently implementing the strategy set by senior management. Clearly, it is equally as critical for an organization to invest time and resources in transitioning this key person into his or her new position and/or new environment, and executives are pivotal to this process. The following five focus areas spell out the necessary ingredients to help executives successfully find, hire, and transition middle managers.

1. *Define the challenge.* The first step to a successful transition is hiring the right person for the job. To accomplish this, executives need to define the goals for that position. What kind of work needs to be done? What skills are needed? For example, a different skill set is needed to turn around a department versus sustaining its performance. Does the department need to move in a different direction? Does it need to perform better? Or does it just need to sustain its current focus? Finding the right person with the requisite talents is key—many times the wrong person is hired for the task, and failure is the result.

Defining the challenge is not as easy as one might think. Making decisions based on perceptions will bring unfortunate results. To truly understand a situation, executives should conduct a 360-degree review of a given department to determine its challenges and the solutions—thereby outlining the correct person to hire for the job. This review involves talking with the executive team, department staff, peer department representatives, and department users such as marketing, sales, finance, logistics, and other managers.

These discussions will identify both positive and negative aspects of the department and may show areas where all participants agree, representing a focal point for the new middle manager. If the results of the review is positive, then it is important to continue the operations as they current exist. If it is negative, then it represents an area requiring attention and improvement.

2. *Define the expectations.* A new middle manager needs a clear explanation of the parameters of his or her new position—an unambiguous understanding of the executive's expectations and definition of success. What needs to be fixed, and what is the time frame to accomplish these tasks? What does success look like? A clear delineation of success, time frames, and performance-related parameters must be communicated between the executive and the middle manager.

These metrics must be definable, known, realistic, and achievable—and sometimes, they must be negotiated between the executive and the middle manager. Although the executive bears the majority of the responsibility in this area, middle managers must be willing to "manage" the executive if these expectations are murky. Executives should do their best to avoid creating uncertain expectations, but managers should be on the lookout for roadblocks, such as mixed messages or obstacles placed in their way.

3. *Define the working relationship.* The path to open communication can be tricky to navigate and doesn't always come with a map. It is up to the executive to provide that map for new middle managers to ensure that the working relationship is a smooth and productive one. Does the executive prefer

- e-mail or voice mail?
- frequent meetings or weekly briefings?
- detailed summaries or just highlights?
- written or oral reports?
- formal or informal agendas?

All of these preferences can make or break a working relationship, and it is important to identify them early to ensure its success.

4. *Identify a mentor within the organization to guide the new manager.* Having a mentor can help middle managers be successful in their positions, especially when transitioning into a new position. Employees will tend to fail or succeed on the informal side of doing business—not based on the skills that they bring to the table.

Whether these individuals are new to the organization or just new to the position, mentors help them navigate through the unfamiliar and point them toward sound decisions based on the culture and needs of the organization, in addition to providing important feedback about the organization. Mentors can teach these managers how things are achieved in an organization— who makes the decisions and why. Mentors also can identify the politics that exist within all organizations.

5. *Hire an outside coach.* Sometimes middle managers have the technical skills to perform a job but do not have the managerial experience to be successful. Using a neutral, outside coach to help that individual acquire the requisite skills needed is an important means to his or her success. Devoting time, resources, and energy to the transitioning of middle managers is a sound investment because actual dollars can be lost through the termination and replacement of a failed manager. Also, additional costs can be accumulated by potential vacancies as an executive struggles to refill that position—costs associated with momentum stoppage, department staff turnover, and loss of employee morale. Finally, an executive should consider how long it will take the new manager to get up to speed and run a productive department. Given the dual challenges of high turnover rates and a shrinking pool of appropriate candidates for these positions, the successful transition of middle managers has never been more important.

Middle managers may possess technical skills, but success in a leadership role requires more than technical competence. It requires organizational communications skills, political and cultural sensitivity, and the ability to get things done through other people. Education will help, but on its own it is not sufficient because success within an organization is only in part due to formal management education. Middle managers, like executives, need support with developing and implementing a transition plan. Organizations should have a formal transition plan to help middle managers acclimate to their new roles.

TALENT MANAGEMENT: HOW TO RETAIN TOP TALENT WITHOUT DERAILING THE ORGANIZATION WHEN FAST-TRACKING

Most people would not choose to build a house on a weak foundation. Why, then, do leaders risk the company's future on an untested, inexperienced employee? To keep him or her motivated, perhaps? To ensure he or she stays with the company?

But at what cost to the employee, the employees who work for him or her, and the company?

Yes, if you want to retain your top employees, you must

- give them a reason to stay;
- find a way to motivate them;
- reward them.

In order for companies to retain top talent and stay competitive in today's market, they are engaging in fast-tracking. This means they are moving selected employees quickly to or through managerial levels in an organization. But, if you reward too much, too fast—it can be dangerous for your entire organization.

Five Reasons Why Fast-Tracking Is a Dangerous Strategy for Increasing Employee Retention

1. *Skills can be learned quickly; experience takes time.* In order to be an effective leader, your managers need to gain experience in
   - correctly identifying and solving problems;
   - framing and making good decisions;
   - dealing with the myriad of people-related issues that confront every manager in every organization;
   - organization course-correction;
   - role-based leadership.
2. *Many times, when your organization engages in fast-tracking, a new manager will set a new initiative in motion and then leave the position before the impact of the initiative is realized.* He or she is missing the day-to-day experience of interpersonal behaviors and interactions that come with any transition—the intangibles. It's these subtleties that are often missed. And it's these subtleties—and the way they are handled—that hone a good leader.

3. *Each managerial level brings new challenges and requires different skills and behaviors.* Moving too quickly through an organization runs the risk of missing critical experiential learning. Experience is accretive, and it is difficult to learn vicariously. What you learn today you use as a framework for how you behave and react tomorrow. Short-changing this learning cycle can result in a leader derailing later.

4. *When leaders derail because a company engaged in fast-tracking in order to retain top talent, it creates a disastrous domino effect for the organization as a whole.* We all know that the number-one reason people leave a company is because of their immediate supervisor. We also know that poor decisions and poor problem-solving skills can result in a deterioration of service and profitability for the entire company.

5. *Fast-tracking creates a winner/loser environment within the company.* Unless you want to build a highly-competitive, stressful environment and internal culture that makes your employees hate Mondays, creating winners and losers is not a good long-term strategy.

Why Companies Engage in Fast-Tracking, Even though It's Dangerous to the Health of the Organization

Companies need to grow talent internally and ensure smooth management transitions. But the reality is that some industries are disproportionately affected by talent shortages (such as health care) and may have no other choice than to promote an employee who is truly not ready to handle the position. (This is a common practice for technical and clinical staff who are promoted to management.)

So what should you do?

Seven Tips for Retaining Top Talent without Hurting Your New Manager, Employees, and the Company

1. *Develop a succession plan for your company.* This means get committed to a process or structure of internal management and talent development.

2. *Identify individuals within the organization who have the potential to move into leadership positions.* You should be identifying multiple candidates for each position. Don't be afraid to take some risks in candidate identification. Not all high-potential candidates initially present an outgoing and aggressive demeanor (and remember these qualities do not necessarily ensure a good manager).

3. *Provide the identified individuals with opportunities to take on additional projects to demonstrate their skills as well as their ability to learn and grow.* The projects should create the opportunity for the candidates to "live" with the consequences and take responsibility for their actions and decisions.

4. *Provide new managers with an internal mentor or an external coach to ensure support during the transition process.* This support should be in place for at least six months to one year. This process is referred to as "transition integration."

5. *Give all new managers a personality and job performance assessment.* This is a valuable tool in identifying emerging leader attributes and potential risk areas. Now you will be able to enable early intervention and prevention and give the most effective support to the new manager. This is better than the "sink or swim" approach to learning that new managers are often thrown into.

6. *Provide all candidates with self-assessment tools and learning opportunities.* Do this both from within the organization in the form of added responsibilities, and through outside learning opportunities such as conferences, executive education programs, and professional memberships.

7. *Monitor your new manager's progress (through the supervisor and mentoring and coaching support) and review your succession plan each year.* Evaluate the success of the current program and the individuals in the program. Improve where necessary, and identify and support new leadership candidates.

Be aware that some candidates simply may not be interested in this more protracted and performance-based approach. They may feel threatened or choose to leave. That's okay, too. The risk of promoting too quickly and the derailment that could occur is not worth the harm an unprepared manager can bring to the organization.

Talent is to be developed, not anointed.

CHAPTER

9

PUTTING IT ALL
TOGETHER

While we were writing this book, we were interviewed by a writer for a magazine that was doing a story on SMB organizational performance and improvement. He asked us the same question that others ask: Where do you start?

This is a fair question, and it's an important question. The quick answer—which admittedly seems to lack satisfaction and feels a bit like you are Alice in Wonderland, yet is the critical key to begin work on becoming a gravitational organization—is start from where you are now.

WHAT'S YOUR CURRENT STATE?

Let's explain. Every business we work with and every business owner and executive we talk to has a current state. This current state is very likely to be different for each of them:

- good brand—poor delivery
- good delivery capability—poor brand recognition
- brand ambiguity—inconsistent delivery
- no brand expression—poor cost control
- no brand expression—excellent cost control
- poor brand expression—poor delivery—poor cost control

We could go on, and we encourage you to add the current situation that exists for your business to the list above. Yes, what we find is that all businesses have a distinctive situation. Until that situation is identified and understood, moving toward building a gravitational organization is an exercise in futility.

How do you identify your current situation? You start with the strategy initiative outlined in Part One. Strategy begins with identifying your current state, and, if done well, it involves a brutally honest assessment of where you are today and why.

In the Appendix, we provide a self-assessment questionnaire: Organizational Gravity Assessment Worksheet. The worksheet asks a series of questions to help you determine how you and your business are performing on the four organizational gravity areas: strategy, brand, culture, and talent. Your answers will provide a guide to where you should focus your improvement efforts.

As described in chapter 1, the strategy process has a beginning, middle, and kick-off point.

The process we use when we work with businesses involves these steps:

- Interviews with key executives to determine their perceptions of the organization. Where is it now, and why? How do they feel about their position in the organization and the organization's future? Additional questions we ask:
  - o What are your biggest recent successes?
  - o What are your biggest challenges?
  - o Who are your customers?
  - o What are your differentiators?
  - o How are your customers better off because they do business with you?

- o Are you on target?
- o What is your three- to five-year vision?
- o What are the top three priorities for your organization?
- o Do you (and your people) have the resources needed to adequately fulfill your responsibilities and targets?
- Review of relevant company data and information, including information such as these:
  - o Brand items, including website and other social media initiatives and marketing collateral
  - o Financial history and performance
  - o Past strategic initiatives and success with implementing them
  - o Sales strategy
  - o People plan (organizational chart, succession plan, talent acquisition and retention)
  - o Employee satisfaction assessments/climate study findings
  - o Performance appraisal process
  - o Customer surveys/feedback

This information provides a good assessment of where the organization is today.

A STORY OF MISALIGNMENT

A company in the manufacturing business wanted an assessment of where it was. The objective was to see if the executives were aligned.
In conducting this exercise, the results were revealing:

- The CFO believed that the company was doing okay, and her main objective was to grow it and cash out in less than five years.
- The chief sales officer was working with large corporate buyers to sell a new line of solid product. (The company at the time made only a liquid version.)

- The head of manufacturing was focusing on getting a new plant online. (The current plant produced liquid product only.)

This list is just a snapshot of what we found. But as you can see, the executive team was not only misaligned; they were, in fact, working at counter purposes. Moving forward with such a misaligned executive team could not happen. The president and CEO essentially had only two choices: realign the executive team or replace the executive team. Until the alignment issue was addressed, progress was not possible. The president eventually chose to replace some of the executive team members.

We don't often find executive teams that have such large differences in their perspectives about the company, its products/services, and its direction. But when this occurs, there is a clear need for leadership. And that leadership rests squarely on the CEO's shoulders. No one else in the organization can effectively pull off realignment. If the CEO doesn't get it or can't do it, the chairman of the board must step in and replace the CEO. If this is an entrepreneurial venture, and there is no board, then the organization will suffer, be marginalized in the market, and close. At the very least, your good talent will go elsewhere.

In an organization such as the one we described above, the potential for attracting and retaining top talent is virtually zero. This is not a case of good people not being available in the market; it's a case of good people not wanting to work for a toxic or fading organization.

SELF-ASSESSMENT, SELF-AWARENESS, AND MOVING FORWARD

This is why self-assessment and self-awareness is so important. Without it, improvement is just a stochastic event. As the old saying goes, even a blind squirrel finds a nut every now and then, but it doesn't mean he knows what he's doing.

When you understand where you are—your current situation—you are now ready to plan your next move.

Since it is impossible for us to know your current condition, we provide a general outline of how you should think about improvement. Since these are sequential steps, you can enter at the point that is most relevant to you and your current situation.

If, however, you are struggling in all areas, we recommend these steps first:

1. Ensure that you provide cost-effective, high quality delivery to your customers/clients
2. Ensure that you have the leadership team to deliver it

A significant disconnect occurs when delivery is poor yet the promise is grand—and the current executive team doesn't truly understand this represents a disconnect.

To reiterate, the general approach to improving your current condition and positioning for growth is to

- understand executive team alignment;
- understand how you are perceived in the market;
- understand your internal efficiency and company climate (i.e., culture and employee perceptions);
- understand your financial performance and financial efficiency.

Once you understand this, take the following steps:

- Fix the internal issues (infrastructure) first—culture/financial performance.
- Clearly define what you will provide for your customer (product/service) and align your brand messaging.
- Clearly understand your ability to follow through on what you will provide your customer.
- Clearly understand the financial implications, and be certain that you can financially support your plan.
- Start executing.

We place fixing the internal issues first for a reason. Unless you can deliver on your promise to your customer, you are likely to lose customers because you can't deliver. And do remember, your employees are internal customers.

IMPLICATIONS ON TALENT

Another reason for fixing the internal issues first is so you can draw talent. Sure, you don't have a good brand yet, but you have an awareness of your current state. You have a plan to address it and grow, you know how you want to position your product or service, and you have an idea of how you want to create your brand expression. Why is this important? It's important because there is talent in the market who relish and thrive on a challenge, such as the one presented by your company.

You need to position the candidate as becoming part of something great—the turnaround, the improvement, and the rewards that will result in terms of growth, promotion, money, and recognition. You have a great story to tell, and you know exactly where you stand, what you need to do, and who you need in order to do it.

The companies we see as great now all started small. All of them had challenges, and all needed top talent to help them grow: Apple, Microsoft, Facebook, Twitter, and on and on. So it clearly can be done; others have done it. And so can you.

Let's again take a look at the triangle introduced in the first chapter.

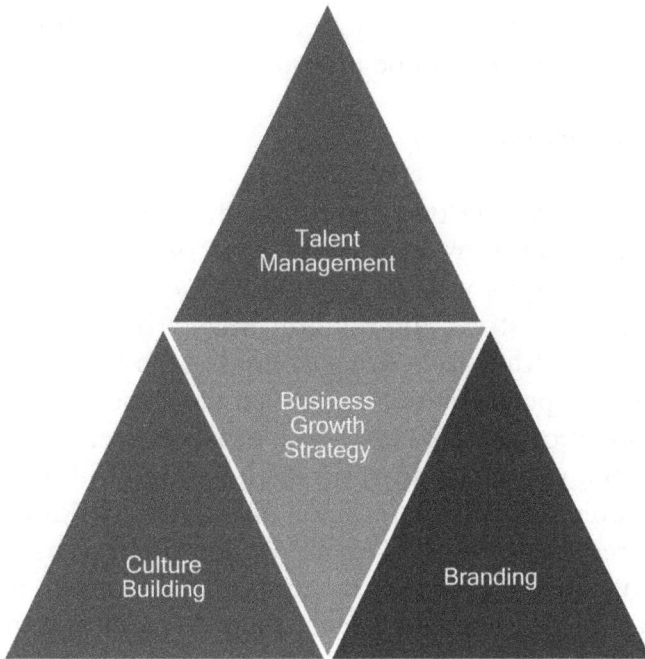

To become a gravitational organization—to become an organization that wants to grow; to become an organization that you want to position to support your exit strategy—four key elements are required:

1. A clear brand expression—an unambiguous expression of your promise to your customer
2. A culture that can support that promise—a culture than can deliver
3. Talent—people who are by your side to help make it happen
4. Strategy to bring it all together

Your business is important. It's important to you, and it's important to others. Customers rely on you for your products/services, employees rely on you for their livelihood, and you are very likely relying on your business to help support your retirement. Building a healthy, growing company and doing what needs to be done does not have to be a daunting challenge. It just needs to start and be attended to.

Your Call to Action:

This book was written for the individuals who are serious about starting and growing a business; who feel something is just not working as well as it could in their business; who feel their business is stuck and not growing as they believe it should grow. It was written to help individuals who have tried change management, performance improvement, social media initiatives, motivational speakers, and other current and popular interventions yet have ended up disappointed in the results.

This book uses the metaphor of gravity, making the point that the greater the mass of an object (and in this case the object is your business) the greater its gravitational attraction. In business what do you want to attract most? Talent and customers. The model and metaphor describe how to build organizational mass through strategy, brand, culture, and talent.

Remember from basic physics that the body (e.g., company) does not necessarily have to be big in size. It can be small but also have a high density. In the business context, high density would be a very well-defined, high-demand product or service offering, and that does not have to end up being a multimillion dollar company. These businesses are present within every community and can be found in successful IT companies, web designer companies, software application development companies, financial firms, insurance companies, and local restaurants, to name just a few. One factor they all have in common is they are gravitational organizations.

Our challenge to you is to take a hard look at your company, using the perspective and ideas presented in this book.

- Are you where you want to be? And do you have an executable plan to get you there?

- Have you balanced your promise with the ability to deliver on your promise?
- Do you have talented people who want to work for you?
- Are you a business that people just want to, and prefer to, do business with?

If not, you can be. You can be by taking the necessary steps to become a gravitational organization.

To your success and fulfillment along the journey.

BONUS SECTION

LEADERSHIP

LEADERSHIP FOR ORGANIZATIONAL GRAVITY

Organizational gravity draws both talent (employees) and customers to your business. We know from high school physics that bodies attract with a force proportional to their mass. Likewise in business, companies attract talent and customers with a force proportional to their organizational mass. Instead of rock or gas, organizational mass consists of a strong brand, a strong culture, talented employees, and a business growth strategy.

Leadership has the responsibility to build and capitalize on the interrelationships of strategy, brand, culture, and talent to build a gravitational organization. And leadership is about:

- you – your confidence, your skill, your presentation when showing up; and self-awareness is key to your effectiveness;
- vision and anticipation – your ability to anticipate market need and spot opportunities and threats to create and course-correct the vision/strategic direction of the company;
- alignment – your ability to find common ground and generate collective ambition;
- core values – having and living high standards and guiding principles;
- motivation and empowerment – your ability to inspire and empower those around you;

- challenging – your own and others' thinking - and the status quo;
- awareness – of what is *really* happening in the organization and active attention to influencing it positively;
- action – the ability to make timely decisions and doing something about those decisions.

Talented executives with a talented team of employees are a disruptive force in the marketplace. Executives bring the strategic vision, and employees create both pragmatic and innovative ways to execute the strategy.

Consider the factors that relate to leadership and issues that are important for leaders in building and leading a "gravitational organization."

As the executive, there are eight critical elements that you are responsible for:

1. Ensuring your executive team provides a clear and concise strategic vision and commonly understood purpose for the company with accompanying core values—attitudes, behaviors and beliefs—that drive collective efforts
2. Actively attending to alignment between members of the executive team in developing the strategy and in leading it
3. Ensuring performance accountability in each executive member (and his or her ability to build and work with a strong team if he or she has employees/ departments)
4. Ensuring that interpretation (communication) of the strategy and key priorities cascade from the executives through the middle managers to the staff
5. Providing strategy implementation guidance and support that ensures the authority and autonomy of your employees to carry out their work
6. Ensuring the executive team puts customer-centric growth and retention strategies in place using employee *and* customer feedback and ideas

7. Ensuring a brand strategy and respective brand messaging/tactics that encapsulates your market and your distinct value (competitive advantage)
8. Ensuring there is a succession plan in place for all critical positions/levels of your business. This is an interrelated element for business growth and talent management and development of your next generation of leaders.

No business is perfect. Growth is complicated and stressful. Providing strategic leadership and direction by setting and messaging a clear strategy and priorities, by understanding, making, and keeping promises to your customers and your employees, and by empowering your employees to consistently contribute their best will grow and distinguish your business.

LEADERSHIP QUALITIES/QUALIFICATIONS: ONE DEBATE THAT'S IRRELEVANT

There is a debate about what qualities/qualifications CEOs should have. Should they be marketers, rainmakers, financial experts, or people experts? This argument is irrelevant and useless. In today's economy, you need to be a great strategist, be financially savvy, have strong marketing acumen, understand logistics, understand how to use technology to leverage business growth, and be able to work with people. And as long as the discussion is focused on one person possessing all these skills, or on which of these skills is most important, the critical task of running a successful business will be missed— and the selection process will fail far more often than it succeeds.

Even small businesses face similar issues as they begin to grow. A solo entrepreneur may do literally everything in the business, but as the business grows, what was once a strength now becomes a major impediment to the growth, if not the survival, of the business.

A CEO is like a conductor of an orchestra. Does anyone seriously care if the conductor has a background in piano or violin? It doesn't matter. What matters is whether the conductor can get the various musicians—which have major and minor roles depending on the piece being played—to play their parts exceedingly well. That's the job of the conductor; that's the job of the CEO.

One of the most important decisions a board can make is hiring a CEO who is capable of building and working with a strong team. If you run a small company and do not have a board, one of the most important decisions you will make is to hire a strong and complementary team. And it's not just the executive team that's important; the department heads and key managers and supervisors are also important. Executives set strategy; middle managers execute strategy.

Business success never has and never will depend solely upon one person with one skill set for success.

LEADERSHIP STARTS FROM WITHIN

Leaders create and run successful companies. Leaders also destroy companies. What we've found is that far too many leaders create problems and negative challenges for their organizations and staff, and they do so without realizing it. In fact, they often think they are doing the right things and behaving correctly.

David Doltich and Peter Cairo wrote a book called *Why CEOs Fail*[1], and Marshall Goldsmith wrote a book titled *What Got You Here Won't Get You There*[2]. The themes are the same. Whether we call it self-sabotage, derailers, or annoying habits, they are behaviors that can prevent your organization from succeeding.

Common examples include the following:

- lack of (timely) responsiveness
- inability to build and maintain relationships
- arrogance
- perfectionism
- spouting (versus speaking) when angry
- playing favorites
- using monologue versus dialogue with others

What makes it even more difficult is that the very behaviors that are causing you problems as a leader may be the same behaviors that resulted in you becoming a leader. We have all heard the phrase "our greatest strengths can become our greatest weaknesses." And so it is.

What we are describing can blindside you. It is very difficult to understand that what worked so well for you in the past is now one of your greatest risk factors.

Want to know if you have a tendency toward self-sabotage? Or should we say, do you have the courage to find out?

Consider doing the following:

- Take a business personality assessment that focuses on leadership style.
- Reflect on the times when you were unsuccessful—when you failed to achieve your goal. What patterns can you identify?
- Ask your direct reports.
  - o This is very powerful and can provide the best feedback and information to you. But you must create a safe environment for them. Remember, no real relationship—no trust, no risk, and vulnerability.
  - o If you doubt this, think about the times you wondered why your boss couldn't see in himself/herself what was so obvious to everyone else.
- Ask a trusted advisor or colleague.

If you are truly serious about becoming a more effective leader and running a successful company, start first by looking at and within yourself. Other people's behavior may be nothing more than a coping mechanism to deal with you. So start with the source.

LEADERSHIP: CLOSING THE LEARNING—PERFORMING GAP

Can you get better by reading a book, listening to podcasts, or going to seminars? This question makes for a vibrant debate for many who claim they can; however, the real reason people improve is because they *do* something about it. That is, they take action.

We've all heard variations on the definition of insanity: doing the same things over and over again and expecting different results. Leadership development is much the same. A training day here, a workshop there, and presto—leaders are developed. Well—it's just not so.

And why would it be? Let's think about it for a moment. As a business owner, the last thing you are is the same as every other business owner. Your market is different; your opportunities are different; your culture is different; your team's skills and interactions are different. Some of you are in a business formation stage; others are transitioning business models or business focuses to capitalize on the new realities of business (post-Great Recession). Some of you are building teams; some of you have well-established teams. Some of you, unfortunately, believe that nothing has really changed, and you are slowly trying to get back to business as usual. One size does not fit all; one approach is not relevant to all businesses.

A study on the effectiveness of leadership development initially published by Marshall Goldsmith and Howard Morgan in the magazine *Business+Strategy* in Fall 2004, which first involved 86,000 respondents, has since been updated to include more than 250,000 respondents. Their conclusion: "Very few people achieve positive, lasting change, without ongoing follow-up." And the follow-up the authors are referring to is with colleagues and coaching support. We reference this as learning integration or learning transference. If you are not sure this makes sense, honestly answer the following question: Can you improve your physical fitness and health by reading a book? We can't, and our guess is that you can't either. We need to know not only what to do, we need to do it, and we need the support, encouragement, and lessons from those around us to continue doing it. Leadership development is no different.

Leadership development is a process, not an event. It's the difference between getting the training and using the training to improve. Getting the training is an event (with a very short retention half-life, by the way). Using the training is a process that involves daily application, working with and getting feedback from your colleagues, and coaching support. Furthermore, it's a customized process that reflects the learning style of those involved.

YOUR PERSONAL ENERGY IMPACTS YOUR LEADERSHIP

"Is she in a good mood this morning?" "Man, I wonder what's bugging him today."

We all recognize this. It's the "boss watch." If the boss is in a good mood and upbeat, the day goes much better than if the boss is on a tirade. Yes, bosses (you as well) have an impact on the mood and productivity of the organization. When you exude confidence and positive energy, the organization responds in kind. When you are negative, evasive, and cautious, the organization picks this up and responds in kind. You, as a leader, impact the mood of the organization, and this is referred to as energy leadership.

This is not a new-age gimmick. Think about it. When the boss is upbeat, confident, and has good, concise, and believable answers to your concerns about the business and the market—how do you feel? Pretty good. If, on the other hand, the boss is competing with Eeyore (of A. A. Milne fame) for the most laconic award, how do you feel then? Pretty poor—perhaps even discouraged. This is the essence of how your energy impacts your leadership.

It is important for you, as the leader, to realize the impact you have on the organization by your mood; in other words, your energy—the energy you present and (knowingly or unknowingly) share with others. We find lack of awareness (and for some, believability) is a major issue here. These folks say that the idea that their energy could be a factor in their leadership style is ridiculous and laughable. Well, it certainly isn't ridiculous or laughable to their employees, who experience poor clarity, negative anticipation, and may begin to even avoid their negative-energy boss. This contributes to a less-than-favorable reputation for both the employer and the company and will ultimately negatively impact productivity. A high price to pay for ignoring the obvious, don't you think?

We are coming out of a recession and facing a difficult and sluggish recovery in some market sectors. Executives are looking for ways to reinvigorate their businesses, reenergize their staff, and identify and refocus on emerging market opportunities. None of this is possible in a moribund organization. And you, as the leader, have complete control over this.

A Note on Executive Presence (Impression Management)

Have you ever seen one of those T-shirts that says, "It's not how you play the game that counts, but how you look while you're playing the game"? Well, at least they got part of it right. How you look *does* influence the majority of people's interpretation of you. We have about thirty seconds to make a first impression, and that first impression (positive or negative) is generally lasting. And this is generous, as many experts say that first impressions are made within the first ten seconds.

But it takes more than looking good if you want to be truly effective in business. We all know the people who absolutely look great—well-groomed, well-dressed. And that's it; that's all they've got. "They" are pejoratively referred to as "empty suits." Executive presence is more than the Armani suit, the Chanel leather portfolio, and the Rolex watch. We believe that it's about *being* the part. It's about your knowledge and skills, *and* your self-confidence and self-esteem.

Executive presence is about preparing yourself and, yes, taking care of yourself. People with low self-esteem (and this is an issue for some regardless of the positions they hold) and low self-image often neglect their health and their appearance. We are not talking about looking like the models in *GQ* or *Vogue*; we are talking about having suitable and appropriate self-respect.

Like it or not (yes, we know this is a very sensitive area, but we are committed to candidness and performance support), tired, overweight, out-of-shape, and sloppy people present a very different image than people who take care of themselves.

And please don't kill the messenger.

We are also talking about preparing and growing yourself. What you read, who you listen to, and what you watch on television contributes to who you are as a person. Building relationships, which is a key part of what you do as a leader, is dependent in part on finding common ground. Involved, informed people like to know they are talking to involved, informed people—not just a phantasm wrapped up in a nice suit.

So, if this resonates with you, here are some key points for you to consider:

- unplug—the more you are on your smartphone, the *less available* you are to those around you. You are missing opportunities!
- look at and connect with those around you—be willing to smile at others, look them in the eyes, and hear what they have to say.
- match your dress to the client's situation.
- read—be familiar with current events, bestsellers, and community events relevant to the client.
- use intelligent words; sound intelligent (and be prepared to discuss your reasoning and opinion if asked!).
- take care of yourself—get adequate sleep, exercise, and practice good nutrition (this includes hydration).
- speak confidently and don't end sentences as if you are asking a question (unless, of course, you are asking a question).

- be aware of annoying and distracting habits. If you are uncertain what yours are, have someone you know and trust point them out to you.
- ask provocative questions.
- carry yourself with confidence and as if you care about what you are doing. (We believe you do, so show it!)
- get help if you feel you are not presenting well—a performance coach or image consultant can work wonders for you.
- act like a peer, regardless of whom you are talking to.
- be interested more than interesting. You don't have to be an amazing conversationalist to talk with others and form new relationships—you just have to be interested in them, and you do this by asking meaningful questions and acknowledging that you're listening and understanding. For example, say, "That's very interesting—would you tell me more about that?"
- be highly conscious of your personal presentation. We strongly believe that when you look good, you feel better about yourself, and when you feel better about yourself, you will exude more confidence. When you are more confident, it seems easier to extend to others.

OH, YOU MEAN WE HAVE TO DO IT? ACCOUNTABILITY MATTERS

Planning can be fun—at least most of the time. The executive team or management group gets together and talks about what is and what could be for the company.

And here's how the process usually goes:

- you look at the current state of the company.
- you discuss and spend time on the daily issues and microissues within the company (also known as "sidebar conversations").

- you start looking at what you need to do as a company.
- you create a list of all the things you *must* do—usually on a white board or flip chart. The list is long because there is so much to do.
  - o oftentimes, the list of "must dos" is not based on actual data (employee surveys, client/customer surveys, or market research—but on the general impressions of the people in the room).
  - o you assign people's names to tasks.
  - o everyone walks out with his or her list.

Next day, the employees go back to their jobs, and it's business as usual. There may be a few follow-up meetings. But the reality is that there is way too much day-to-day work to do.

And here are snippets of conversations we hear in the meetings, during the breaks, and afterward back on the job:

- how can we possibly do all this when I have too much to do already?
- things really aren't going to change around here—it's just the same ole, same ole.
- tell me what I shouldn't do.
- these actions really won't help, and I don't think they are worth spending my time on (usually uttered by people who disagreed with the conclusions and the go-forward action plans).
- if I do what they propose, I'll be out of a job (frequently a complete misconception).

And another year passes.

What we've just described are businesses that lack discipline, focus, and effective leadership. These businesses may or may not be affected by the economic conditions in the marketplace, but they are all infected with a disease we made up called *complacertiaosis* (a combination of complacency and inertia).

Now, just to be fair, there are organizations that do an outstanding job with planning. They do it the right way, and their follow-through is exceptional. These are usually the more successful companies.

For a business owner or executive, planning—and then implementing the necessary changes to realize the plan—takes thoughtfulness, time, leadership, and courage. And your people, the ones who will be charged with implementing your plan, are by far the potential weak link in the planning chain. How you prepare them, how you support them, and how you reward them will directly relate to how successful you are. Miss this, and you have wasted money, wasted time, disrupted the organization, and maintained business as usual.

ACCOUNTABILITY — A GROWTH FACTOR

Do what you say you will do, when you say you will do it, to get the results expected—without having to be prodded, reminded, or rewarded. Sounds pretty simple and straightforward—right? Well, not exactly.

We find too many examples in business of "Yes, I'll get that done—no problem," followed by missed deadlines and sometime ingenious excuses or avoidance. The bottom line is a promise not delivered, a deadline not met, and business results not yet achieved.

Accountability is not something the boss asks for (or requires) and the subordinate complies with or negotiates. Accountability is not dependent on whether you are the boss, peer, or subordinate. It is not positional. Accountability is a value and shows up as a personal trait. It is who you are—not what or who you are told to be. Some people have it naturally; others acquire it; and many (in our experience) don't really believe it is that important, as demonstrated by their actions speaking louder than their words.

You cannot effectively build or grow a small business if even one person does not hold himself accountable for results. Larger businesses are also impacted, but the layers of redundancy can hide it for a while, though at a great cost to the business—and to its customers.

Partnerships and small businesses by definition and economic reality are small and resource-constrained. To support growth, everyone must contribute without being told what to do or when to do it. If the latter does not occur, there may be a tendency to hire another person to pick up the slack. This is a wrong solution. Quick correction of the unaccountable individual—or ultimately, replacement of him or her—is the right solution.

So, in business, how do you get an *A* in accountability? Self-accountability means holding yourself accountable to produce results daily (and expecting it of your coworkers as well).

Accountability has other beneficial effects: it increases the energy and excitement about your work, and as you complete more and produce more results, you build confidence. Accountability builds trust as well—three critical ingredients to business growth, especially in the early years.

Accountability is about a personal choice. Ultimately, accountability shows up as a steadfast reliability with—and to—others.

Being accountable will "promote" you, as your word and work will speak to it. This will differentiate you from many others (the "talkers" versus the "make it so'ers"). And people will extend you trust and more opportunities. For businesses and organizations, individual accountability is a driver for producing results. And naturally, when you are accountable, there is a draw to improve in what you are doing, which lends to growth. We call it the cycle of accountability.

FIVE PREREQUISITES IN EMPLOYEE PERFORMANCE ACCOUNTABILITY

Have you done everything that you need to do to support your employees' performance before you hold them accountable for their under-performance?

Following are five critical elements that leaders are responsible for to establish accountability in their employees:

1. *Clear Expectations.* Have you discussed your expectations of the job and the employee's performance with him or her? If there is a performance concern, have you clearly identified the issue(s)?

2. *Opportunity for Training and Development.* Does the employee have the knowledge and skills required to do the job he or she was hired for? If not (and you choose to keep him or her), he or she needs help to learn it. Common options include professional training seminars, in-house training, a mentor for technical assistance and guidance, or an external coach to help get him or her from where he or she is now, to where he or she needs to be.

3. *Address Barriers to Performance.* Does the employee have the necessary resources to perform? For example, does he or she lack proper equipment or workspace? Is he or she limited in his or her authority to get the job done? Could he or she be receiving conflicting messages or instructions from layers of management?

4. *Provide Constructive Feedback.* Have you/are you providing regular (not once a year) feedback on how the employee is performing? Feedback should be frequent, timely (to the situation), specific, honest, and constructive (solution-oriented) in nature.

5. *Deliver Consequences.* Employees need and deserve to know that there are consequences for poor performance and what that may include, and you need to ensure you carry out the consequences if you want to see change and ensure accountability. No consequences equals no accountability, which results in turf wars, infighting, and under-performance.

Mid-Level Management: Remember — Most Employees Leave Their Bosses, Not Their Companies

In this book on organizational gravity, we addressed branding, culture, talent management, and business growth and strategy. If you do a good job at these, you actually may be able to recruit and retain great employees and grow your business.

Now, using a football analogy, good teams play the full sixty minutes and know how to score in the red zone (twenty yards out from the goal). The quarterback can drive his team down the field brilliantly, but unless he can close it out by scoring, it's a missed opportunity.

We think about leadership as playing in the red zone. It's at the interface between the manager and the managed that you either engage the employee, or the employee leaves. In football parlance, you either score or turn the ball over.

Research shows that the number-one reason people leave their jobs is because of their boss. Even in great organizations, there are bad bosses. And here's some help to make sure that you are not one of them.

The principle: A successful manager/managed relationship is bi-directional.

As the supervisor/manager, it is critical for the employee that you

- explain your management style, your key expectations, and how you would like to work with your new employee;
- establish a communication protocol: how often, through what media, and the level of detail expected;
- be consistent;
- be open to the employee's ideas and supportive of his or her learning (you are responsible to help your new employee succeed);
- provide ongoing feedback and mini performance appraisals regularly. The best bosses hold regular one-on-one meetings with their employees and focus on their development;

- don't make ridiculous or incongruent statements such as "I need you to work 24/7 on this," or "I need 110 percent";
- demonstrate leadership.

The manager/managed relationship is a work in progress. And it starts with awareness—the awareness that it's important and that it's a two-way relationship that is worth the time it takes to get it right.

Even as a leader, you may be a subordinate and have a manager. Below, we offer the second half of the formula—for the managed. There are also seven critical actions for you to take in establishing a strong relationship with your boss:

- understand your boss's preferred working style and conform to it, or negotiate something that can work for both of you. This may mean you need to reach out and solicit this conversation if it is not offered to you, as this is a fundamental building block to the positive boss/ employee relationship.
- communicate as agreed to with regard to frequency, media, and level of detail.
- be consistent.
- be supportive both in meetings and in conversations with colleagues and subordinates.
- work hard to de-personalize feedback. Be open, objective, and unemotional—ask for clarification and ideas on how your performance can be improved.
- provide honest feedback to your boss when asked. If you are not asked, do your best to create a conversation and share your key ideas and concerns. For example, say something like, "Boss (insert name), I've got a few important (or sensitive) items I'd really like to discuss with you; can we arrange a time to talk?"
- demonstrate leadership.

It's not enough to expect the relationship between you and your boss will evolve naturally. Sure, evolution works, but as we see in nature, it takes millions of years—time we just don't have. So a nudge, an intervention, some proactive behavior is required. All relationships require work; all good relationships are bi-directional. Our point is to urge you to do your part.

"But" Deteriorates Performance

How you manage your people, how you recognize them, how you encourage them, and how well you do at making them feel appreciated is an important leadership characteristic.

In *How to Win Friends and Influence People* by Dale Carnegie (1940), he tells the story about why Andrew Carnegie paid Charles Schwab a million dollars a year. He paid him that vast sum of money (remember, this was the late 1800s) because of his ability to deal with people.

Charles Schwab says it best in his own words:

> I consider my ability to arouse enthusiasm among the men the greatest asset I possess, and the way to develop that in a man is by appreciation and encouragement. There is nothing else that so kills the ambitions of a man as criticism from his superiors.

Yet criticism often predominates in business. And it shows itself by focusing primarily on what didn't go well or what the person could do better—or by saying a few sentences of something positive and supportive and then moving quickly into what didn't go well. And, of course, it is usually prefaced by that powerful three letter word—"but." "But" is used as an opposing proposition. So, once the word "but" is uttered, everything you just said is quickly forgotten as the person now braces for your "constructive criticism." "But" erases what came before it.

We do not advocate flattery, let alone artificial recognition or ignoring the need for improvement in the employee. We do advocate a shift from the imbalance of criticism/appreciation to appreciation/opportunities to improve.

Here are some myths:

- people know what they do well; it's my job to point out what they don't do well.
- why do I need to waste time with appreciation? I'm busy; let's cut to chase and focus on what needs to get better.
- if people can't take the truth, they need to find another job.

We have an important message for you—no one, and that includes you, likes to have the focus be on only what's not going well, as it taints review and assessment experience. If that's all you hear, it has a powerful de-motivating effect that can ultimately result in learned helplessness, loss of confidence, or quitting—and clearly, morale and productivity are impacted, none of which is good for the company or your business.

Delivering helpful versus hurtful feedback is a skill, and a skill most people sincerely can improve upon. This falls into the "emotional intelligence" of the deliverer to best work with the core yet overlooked elements of the emotional management factors on employee performance and development.

BUILDING YOUR EMOTIONAL IQ TO IMPROVE YOUR EMPLOYEES' PERFORMANCE

Emotional IQ has to do with your self-awareness and emotional management to be effective with others; and how you, as a boss, manage performance and promote growth considering the emotional needs of your staff.

Here are *three keys to know and eight things to do* to encourage and recognize employees and to deliver necessary and "receivable" feedback to help them learn and improve, as both are critical for performance growth:

1. KNOW: Recognition (appropriate praise, appreciation, and acknowledgment) is a driver in employee satisfaction and retention. Miss this, and you may see your talent hit the streets.
2. KNOW: Constructive feedback on its own can literally create underperformance in employees due to decreased morale and trust or learned helplessness.
3. KNOW: That delivering constructive yet "receivable" feedback is difficult for most people, and it's highly unlikely that it will be delivered well when you are upset. (Do not give critical feedback when you are out of your "effective zone.")

1. DO: Work to balance positive and constructive feedback—both are developmental feeders. Simply said, this means ensuring you are giving appropriate positive feedback in addition to what didn't work and needs to improve.
2. DO: Regularly give feedback, both positive and constructive—and not just once a year with a formal performance evaluation. (Meaning, there should be no surprises to the employee at his or her performance review.)
3. DO: Be very aware of your choice of language and tone in delivering feedback.
4. DO: Use feedback as an opportunity to build a relationship and trust. Help the employee understand performance concerns by talking with him or her, recognizing the problem, understanding company policy, and establishing the next steps for course-correction.
5. DO: Set performance goals that are of interest to and ideally co-created by your employee—not just you. Higher motivation is inherent when an employee takes ownership of his or her goals.
6. DO: Use empathy and manners to convey concern and respect—for example, "I understand...I can appreciate...I respectfully disagree, and here's why..."
7. Do: Ask questions to encourage self-reflection/assessment at the beginning of an improvement conversation. For example, try questions like these:

    a. how do you think you are doing (in respect to this project)?
    b. how do you see yourself getting along with others?
    c. what did you learn? What do you believe could go better next time? (And, what would/will you do to make this happen?)

8. Do: Offer support (as appropriate) by asking how you can assist and by establishing agreement for follow-up.

How you recognize employees, how you encourage them, and how well you do at making them feel valued and appreciated, in addition to how effective you are at delivering constructive feedback, will cause employees' motivation meter to either go up or down.

GRATITUDE HAS A RETURN

Let's now consider gratitude and celebration as they relate to business.

Have you woken up in the morning and the first thought that came into your mind was, *Ugh, I'm not looking forward to work today.* Quickly, all the things that could go wrong with the day are meticulously itemized like a shopping list. It begins a day of a downward spiral that can perpetuate into days, weeks, even years.

Later, as you are falling asleep, you grudgingly admit that the day wasn't that bad after all, but then you spend time reflecting on what *was* bad before you go to sleep. If you experience yourself frequenting these behaviors, you are not only wasting your precious time and energy, you are wasting your career, and you are wasting your life. And you are likely making the lives of others around you miserable.

Edward Sanford Martin (1856–1939) said it well: "Thanksgiving Day comes, by statute, once a year; when really, it can come as frequently as the recognition of gratitude."

Applied to business, we find that gratitude—a recognition and thankfulness of what is right—offers a return. Do you celebrate what's good? What is right in your business? What's right with your employees? What's right with your clients? Gratitude feeds a spirit of optimism, and it fuels resiliency. To paraphrase Newton's first law of motion—a thought in motion tends to stay in motion.

We often see business owners and employees waste opportunities because they are subsumed in "ain't it awful." We saw the president of a manufacturing company refuse to increase the sales and marketing budget for his successful product line because the economy was bad—yet there was no evidence that the economy had any impact on his company or the demand for his products. We've seen partnerships paralyzed because partners focused on what wasn't right in the other partner rather than what was right—and there was plenty to celebrate.

Of course, the choice is always yours on whether you see opportunity or whether you see doom and gloom. If you think it is downright silly to be a bright-eyed optimist, then at least try for balance.

Regularly practicing and acknowledging what is right—celebrating what's working and your achievements—will build morale, confidence, relationships, and forward momentum to produce even greater results.

How do you and your business demonstrate a spirit of gratitude and celebrate what is right?

Motivated, Aligned, and Satisfied Employees Are a Differentiator

Demoralized workers do not do great work. Organizations do not become remarkable with demoralized staff. Customers do not love their experience with demoralized employees. Yet we find managers catalyzing demoralizing behavior every day.

We've seen

- Bank of America announce it will lay off thirty thousand employees;

- the chairman of the board of Yahoo! fire the CEO over the telephone;
- HP fire its third CEO—the latest one lasting eleven months.

And what do workers do when faced with these issues?

- they actively look to leave the company, and the best ones do.
- they hunker down, stay out of the way, and just do what they are told to do, keeping as low a profile as possible.
- they become disruptive.
- they decide to look better than others and do whatever it takes to discredit their colleagues—and, in doing so, interject an "every person for themselves" mentality, which further deteriorates the culture.

And the managers are greatly hindered in their ability to help, basically for two key reasons:

1. Many of them are in exactly the same position as the workers.
2. They tend to discount the good advice of others, meaning power can hinder willingness to listen. And regarding this point, the *Wall Street Journal* (9/19/11) reported that a study published in the November 2011 issue of *Journal Organizational Behavior and Human Decision Processes* found:
   "[T]he more power the employees (managers) had, the less likely they were to take coworkers' advice. The reason: Powerful individuals held inflated confidence in their own judgments, which led them to discount even good advice from others."

So we see poor leadership, demoralized workers, and managers who discount good advice from others. Now the best way to look at this is *that's your competition.* Your competition has a reasonable probability of being a dysfunctional organization. And dysfunctional organizations are not—and cannot be—remarkable.

So, do you know how your employees are doing, what they feel and believe about the organization and their managers (including you)? If you don't, you should! Don't be one of those managers with an inflated confidence who believes he or she has it all figured out. Motivated, aligned, and satisfied employees represent a significant differentiator in the marketplace. How strong is your differentiation?

THE "UNDISCUSSABLES"

Have you ever heard any of these statements before?

- we're glad you're here; we need an outsider's perspective.
- if you have something to say, speak up and say it—we value open communication.

What happened when you tried it? Well, in our experience, it probably didn't work out too well for you. Why? Because there are some issues and situations in organizations that are just not discussable—and discussing them violates an organizational norm. (Yes, even though you were "encouraged" to speak up.)

To improve, organizations need to confront reality—the changing market conditions for their products or services, their position within the market, new competitors who have products and services that are disruptive in the market, poor performers within the organization, and poor systems and processes.

Leaders need to address impediments to organizational improvement. And to do this, they need evidence and the ability to discuss and debate the evidence and make decisions with the intent to improve performance. But when these issues are not discussable, it is impossible to gather evidence. Unfortunately, what end up being gathered are myths—reinforcing how things are just fine or just temporary setbacks.

All organizations (both large and small) are vulnerable. We hear business people say, "We have been successful thus far; there is no reason we won't continue to be successful." These words are spoken as the competition is gaining a foothold in their market (e.g., Wal-Mart's disruptive impact on small-town businesses). Who would ever stand in a "cattle line" to board a plane (spoken by more than one airline about Southwest)? How long did it take the newspaper industry to realize its position in the marketplace was changing forever? We see the book publishing industry scrambling to figure out how to deal with eBooks and the burgeoning self-publishing industry. Clayton Christensen gave us some insights into the consequences of the "undiscussables" in his book the *Innovator's Dilemma (Harvard Business School Press 1997).*

You cannot create innovations nor can you respond to them effectively in an organization where undiscussables exist—or worse, where the mere suggestion that there may be undiscussables is not discussed.

So how do you address the undiscussables in organizations when these issues are undiscussable? Through evidence and gentle persistence.

If you are the CEO and are concerned that the inability to discuss certain issues exists in your organization, we suggest that you test your assumption.

You do this by

- determining how you're positioned in the marketplace (i.e., customer survey);
- assessing how well your internal processes functions;
- conducting a financial risk assessment;
- conducting an employee survey to pulse perceptions.

These actions will provide you with objective evidence about how your company is performing. And for obvious reasons, these tasks should not be performed by anyone working within your organization or by anyone who would like to work in your organization. In truth, doing this takes courage—courage to face what you may not have been willing to face in the past.

If you are not the CEO or owner, your approach will be different. But you have a responsibility (if you believe that the organization is not performing nearly as well as it could) to step forward and raise awareness.

You do this by

- presenting your ideas, plans, recommendations, and suggestions along with solid evidence to support your position;
- not openly challenging your boss or the other senior people in the company;
- being respectfully persistent.

This will enable you to demonstrate improvement opportunities. We advise being respectful and persistent and not challenging leadership openly, for obvious reasons. Senior people get to senior positions in all organizations because they represent the culture. And if the culture supports the undiscussables, challenging them openly can be dangerous to your career. Educating the senior leaders with facts has a chance for success.

Not all leaders will want to do what it takes to succeed. That is simply a business fact. But others will, and they will be the ones who tolerate undiscussables in their organization.

TRUST — MIRROR, MIRROR, ON THE WALL...

Trust. It's the bedrock of business and personal success. Yet we often find when we talk with people about trust, they say, "Of course it's important; if only (fill in the name) would recognize it." Well, this piece is not about someone else; it's about you.

We have yet to talk with someone who said, "You know, I just can't be trusted." We all see ourselves as trustworthy. Our filters carefully sort out those we feel we can trust and those we feel we cannot. But remember, someone else is applying his or her filter to you. How do you measure up? Do you know?

What we call "trust events"—situations that create a trust violation—can range from small and easily resolved (for example, your boss asked if you called a client; you say yes, and then immediately call the client after the conversation ends). Or it can be large and nonrecoverable (such as embezzling money from your employer). Large trust events tend to result in immediate and strong negative feedback. Small trust events don't. But if they are a part of your behavior, they accumulate, and just like a boxer who is throwing body punches for nine rounds, they add up and will lead to major problems. For the boxer—a tenth-round knockout.

We see partnerships dissolve, employees leave organizations, and employees no longer interacting and cooperating in the workplace, all because of trust violations. Billions of dollars of lost productivity, lost opportunities, and suppressed growth can be attributed to trust issues.

We realize it's difficult to self-reflect on an issue as sensitive as trust in the workplace and business. And it's also unrealistic to assume that if someone has a trust issue with you, he or she will tell you. Some will, of course, but most won't. So instead of asking you directly to assess your trust quotient, we suggest you derive it (or test it) based on a series of simple questions:

- are people you once interacted with on the job spending less time with you? Maybe even avoiding you?
- are people who once shared personal stories and talked with you with animation and interest not doing so any longer? Has the conversation turned and stayed matter-of-fact and businesslike?
- are you invited to fewer meetings and events?
- are you losing customers and having a hard time acquiring new ones?
- are calls that once were returned quickly not being returned?

- are e-mails that were once responded to quickly being responded to more slowly and with less information in the response?
- are you being passed over for key projects or a promotion?

If you answered "yes" to these questions, you likely have a trust issue. Now, sure, this could stem from a temporary work overload or stress overload on the other person. However, a pattern of yeses to these questions with various people, and over some time, presents a high likelihood that your trustworthiness is not coming through to others. This pattern calls for attention on your part if you do not wish for your relationships and success to be diminished.

To give you examples of actions you can take to gain and keep trust, we pull from Stephen R. Covey's great book, *The Speed of Trust* (Free Press, 2008), in which he identifies thirteen character and competency behaviors of high-trust leaders. We identify these, and then briefly describe them from our perspective:

1. Talk straight – that is, communicate clearly and clarify agreements to avoid misunderstanding.
2. Demonstrate respect, which is grounded in principles of fairness, kindness, and civility to all, not just those who have influence on/over you.
3. Create transparency – be open and authentic about yourself and agendas.
4. Right wrongs – if you have wronged someone, whether intentionally or unintentionally, be accountable sooner than later. Apologize, clear it, and make it up in some way. No excuses, no defensiveness—override your ego and grow through humility.
5. Show loyalty – be generous with praise, appreciation, and recognition of others and their value.
6. Deliver results - produce consistently.
7. Get better - adopt a lifelong learning and self-development philosophy.

8. Confront reality - "having your head in the sand is not a viable strategy for relationship-building or success."
9. Clarify expectations - create common ground and agreements on direction (and actions) forward.
10. Practice accountability - demonstrate your own by taking responsibility and seeing it through. If you lead others, be clear on how progress is tracked and consequences are delivered. Then uphold the standards and practices.
11. Listen first - you have two ears and one mouth for a reason. The more you hear and the less you assume, the more you will understand the individual.
12. Keep commitments - keep your word. If you must break it (for whatever reason), immediately acknowledge it, apologize if appropriate, and renegotiate the next steps.
13. Extend trust - offer (demonstrate your giving of) trust through first believing others are worthy of it and capable and caring enough to earn and uphold it. You get by giving—not withholding.

A Leader's Edge: Influence without Positional Authority

Can you achieve results without authority? The simple answer is yes. The challenge is how to do it.

Each of us has a limited amount of authority. And the positional authority that comes with our title enables us to have some influence, but far less than what is required to get the work done. In order to be effective in our work, in order to get things done on time and with the quality expected, and in order to meet the demands and expectations of our customers and those with whom we work, we need to rely on others. And to do that, we need influence.

In this section, we describe why influence is important for getting work done. We will also identify who you need to influence and present ideas, thoughts, and suggestions on how to exert influence in a positive and constructive way. We also recognize that you are exposed to ideas on an almost daily basis that are intended to help you do something better: negotiate, delegate, plan, or manage your time. What we've seen in our work is that an improvement idea is presented as something you should do to improve. What sometimes happens, however, is nothing (no action is taken), or action is taken but it doesn't work.

We believe one of the reasons improvement actions do not work as we thought or hoped they would is because the behavioral issues we possess (and may not be aware of) stand in the way of effectively introducing and using the information to our advancement. In other words, we know what we should do; we know why we should do it; and we know it will benefit us, so we try it, it doesn't work, and we stop trying. There is one step missing: understanding the behavior that may be standing in our way. In this section, we introduce this behavior first, and then discuss how you can increase your ability to influence others.

INFLUENCE IS A LEADERSHIP QUALITY AND A MANAGEMENT SKILL

Influence is the ability to achieve our objective (to get work done) when we do not have complete control or enough authority to accomplish our objective. Influence is not manipulation. Done well and done right, influence is also not:

- a demonstration of power;
- a method to gain greater control;
- a way to promote your personal agenda;
- a way to look good to others in the organization;
- a means of self-promotion.

Influence is about mutuality. It's about a positive exchange of value.

ENABLERS AND DISABLERS IN INFLUENCE

While influence is a powerful tool for getting work done (in fact, it is essential for getting work done), there are barriers that can stand in your way of influencing others. Through our research, we have identified ten barriers to influencing others:

1. Fear
2. Inability to develop real relationships
3. Poor responsiveness
4. Overselling
5. Quitting at "no"
6. Perfectionism
7. Overexpressing personal beliefs
8. Lack of focus
9. Poor impression management (executive presence)
10. Lack of gratitude to and recognition of others

We have often found that one or more of these behavioral traits is present in individuals who believe (or who others believe) that they are less successful than they either want to be or can be. These behaviors are the intangibles that can inhibit good performance. And not being able to exert influence results in performance that comes up short of expectations.

We believe these intangibles are so important to recognize and attend to (if you see these in your own thought processes or behaviors) that should you refuse to address them, even if trying every strategy and technique we present, you will still come up short of exerting the influence necessary to get work done.

We also feel these traits are important to discuss because unless you are aware of impediments to better performance, there is a natural tendency to resist and overlook your own behaviors to improve performance and business results. Far too often, we think that education, skills, and experience alone will carry the day. Possessing them will certainly help you get the job, but being effective in the job and keeping the job require attention to the intangibles of job performance. Consider the ten barriers as they commonly, yet subtly, show up in people, managers, and leaders alike.

- *Fear* is the number-one issue that stops us from using influence to get our work done. And fear appears in many forms. It can be the fear of failure, the fear of being rejected, the fear of appearing foolish, or the fear that we are not good enough. Regardless of the specific fear, fear stops us dead in our tracks. We don't succeed; we don't exert influence because we've convinced ourselves before we even start that we may not or will not be successful.

- *Inability to develop real relationships.* People work with people they like; they buy from people they like; they provide support to people they like. To think otherwise is to miss an important component of organizational success. It is impossible to exert influence on someone with whom you have not developed a real and positive relationship.

- *Poor responsiveness.* The quicker you respond, the more responsive you appear. And if response is important to the person you want to influence, you have just made a positive impression on him or her, and have often added value by a giving him or her something he or she was interested in.

- *Overselling* is not just an issue we see in salespeople; it is an issue we see throughout an organization, regardless of an individual's position. Overselling is annoying, and it also communicates uncertainty in your position and in the validity of your position. When a person says yes, and you continue to try to convince him or her—what are you really communicating?

- *Quitting at "no."* Nobody likes rejection, yet "no" is sometimes the response when the timing of the request is wrong (for example, "no, not right now" or "no, I need more information"). Oftentimes, an objection is not a rejection; it's a request for more information and an opportunity for further discussion. Don't let "no" be an immediate lost opportunity.

- *Perfectionism.* Too often, we believe that unless a project, proposal, or request is perfectly framed, it cannot move forward. This is just not true. Perfectionism also sends an unintended message—indecisiveness—and, in the worst case, can create immobilization. While you may believe you are striving for perfection, the other person is wondering what's taking you so long.

- *Overexpressing personal beliefs.* Some managers and executives just can't seem to keep their opinions to themselves. Have you heard a manager criticize his peers or subcontractors with statements such as "They just don't get it"? Another danger is to express personal political or social beliefs, such as "The Democrats' version of health care is socialized medicine," or "Teachers are overpaid, and they underperform." Expressing personal beliefs has a way of tearing through an organization and irritating others, and not in a good way. (By the way, these two examples are examples only and do not reflect our personal beliefs.)

- *Lack of focus.* It's difficult to get work done or to garner much respect if you flit from one project to another, one idea to another, and one strategy to another and finish nothing. Often people will just give up, quit listening, or no longer support your efforts.

- *Poor impression management.* This is not just about looking the part; it's about being the part. It's about managing your image thoughtfully and not artificially. Like it or not, unsuitably presented, tired, overweight, out-of-shape, and sloppy people present a poor and unconvincing image.

- *Lack of gratitude.* People like recognition; they like to know they are appreciated; they like to be noticed in a positive way. Ignore this at your peril. Remember, if you are unwilling or think it's unnecessary to recognize and express appreciation for others, your chance of influencing them is remote.

INFLUENCING STRATEGIES

Now that we have presented the intangible behavioral traits that can impede your performance and ability to influence, we will focus on how you can exert influence. The underlying principle of influence is the law of reciprocity. People have expectations that if they provide you with something of value, they will receive something of value in return. Selfish? Hardly. It's human nature.

The law of reciprocity involves an exchange: a value for value, and it is mutual. To engage the law of reciprocity effectively, you must identify what your recipient values.

We have much more to offer than many of us realize. For example, we can offer the following:

- resources
  - o money/funding, personnel, space
- information
  - o about the competition, industry trends, upcoming changes
- organizational support
  - o providing support at a public meeting for a project or needed resources
- personal support
  - o being available and supportive when a person is stressed, vulnerable, or perhaps just needs someone to listen
- reliability
  - o doing what you say when you say you will do it
- gratitude
  - o saying thank you; expressing appreciation for a person's contribution in a way that is meaningful
- excellence in one's product/service

- o producing beyond the expectation of the other person
- vision
    - o identifying the future direction, portraying excitement and confidence in the future and in the outcome of the project
- rapid response
- recognition of efforts – small wins and big victories
    - o recognizing others in a way that is meaningful to them. It can be an award, a new project assignment, or praise at a public meeting
- visibility
    - o providing the opportunity to have others present; facilitate networking

But, most important is for the offer to be meaningful to the recipient. Just because we think we are providing something of value does not mean the recipient agrees with us. To determine what is meaningful, we need to understand issues such as these:

- what do they need to succeed?
- how are they measured on their performance?
- how are they rewarded? And what is their greatest reward?
- what are their career objectives?
- what are their key concerns? (or fears, if they will share them with you)
- what are the key expectations of their boss, peers, subordinates, and constituents?
- what are their preferences for privacy? (both of the individual and the culture of the organization)
- what are their interests outside the organization?

It becomes clearer now that determining value to others is inherent in building and maintaining real relationships.

We would be remiss if we did not mention influence can be gained through negative behaviors and actions as well:

- withholding recognition
- threatening to quit
- refusing to cooperate (passive-aggressive behavior or lack of team participation)
- going public with an issue

While clearly not a desirable way to behave, we have seen these tactics used in the work environment, and some of you may have experienced these tactics used against you.

There are three additional influencing strategies that are important to mention— building relationships, engaging in healthy conflict, and learning to delegate effectively. Other than the first one, these may not initially be thought of as influencing strategies.

In the section on enablers and disablers to influence, we mentioned the importance of building real relationships. This is essential, as giving something to a person with whom you have no relationship can also lead to skepticism on his or her part and to wondering why you are doing this. Building a real relationship is a core strategy for influence, and it includes these actions:

- recognizing that nothing happens until a relationship is developed
- having the other person's best interests in mind—win-win versus win-lose
- understanding and respecting the other person's work style and key needs/expectations
- understanding and respecting personality differences
- finding areas of mutual interest
- using exchange principles to enhance the relationship

The next strategy for influencing others is learning how to deal with and participate in healthy conflict (this was also discussed in chapter 6) . Is it possible that as you work to influence another person that conflict will arise: they will push back, argue, and disagree? Certainly. Let's face it—some people like to argue, like to negotiate, and like to play the devil's advocate. In other words, "they love a good fight." Take note: conflict is not bad or wrong. Engaged in the right way, conflict is good. In fact, it's not only good, it's essential for growth, development, and avoiding "group think." "Healthy conflict"—that is, vibrant, candid, and honest sharing by the individuals involved—leads to

- expanding ideas and perspectives;
- identifying more options;
- better decisions;
- inclusion (value and contribution) rather than reinforcing exclusion.

Conflict can also be perceived when you get a strong "no" (as we mentioned earlier). Coupled with fear, conflict may stop further efforts to influence. Stopping at that point can be an incorrect assumption and a mistake.

Another key strategy for influence that—like healthy conflict—is not often thought of as an influencing strategy is how we evoke interest from others to participate in or take ownership in the work (for example, a project, committee, or event). We do this in a manner similar to delegating. While delegation has traditionally been considered a supervisory "hand off" (or worse, a "pawn off") of work; delegation—that is, the act of handing off a piece of work or entrusting a task to a particular person— is highly dependent on influence when there is no positional authority. We reference this as "solicited delegation."

So, three key factors to consider when influencing others to step up to bat or support our work initiatives are first, the individual—his or her character, competence (knowledge, skills), and motivations/interests (this is the matching of value); second, the situation's risk—its visibility, cost, and importance; and third, based on the first and second factors, the appropriate level of support you will need to provide to him or her to ensure the ongoing exchange of value.

Influence is a powerful tool for getting work done in an organization. Here are seven keys to achieving influence without authority:

1. Understand that influence is a powerful tool to getting work done.
2. Understand that you have more power to influence than you may believe.
3. Understand and practice the law of reciprocity and mutuality.
4. Build and maintain meaningful ("real") relationships.
5. Recognize (the depth and breadth) of what you have to offer.
6. Identify and do your best to provide what the other person values.
7. Expand your repertoire of influencing skills.

Success in your career requires more than the hard skills we learned in school. Success also requires that we recognize and master the intangibles of successful management. And one of the most powerful intangibles is the ability to influence others. Influence provides leverage, and leverage enables us to garner more support and help than we would ever be able achieve on our own or through positional authority alone.

INNOVATION — THE KEY TO REINVENTION AND REINFORCING AN ENTREPRENEURIAL MOOD IN YOUR BUSINESS

Innovation. It's something that most business leaders talk about and aspire to, but how well do they actually do it? In the changed economy, reinvention is a critical must for businesses to prevail today. Yet we find many leaders are pushing it to the side. Why? Because they are too busy working "in" the business.

To innovate requires active attention to making something even better than it is. It requires assessment, critical thinking, and problem solving to modernize or transform what you already have, do, and offer. Mindful strategy sessions can help business leaders take the time to explore more deeply what's working, what's not, and what else their business can and should be doing.

Another superb route to rooting innovation in your organization is to use your talent—your employees—to help. This is successfully done

- by regularly using an ad-hoc innovation committee comprised of cross-functional employees, assigned to the task of analyzing a particular product or service (challenge or opportunity scenario) and providing a recommendation that represents a competitive advantage for the business.
- to integrate space for employee innovation directly into day-to-day business functions, through designating a period of time (weekly or monthly) that employees are free to work on and develop their own (or peers') novel ideas and projects for the business's advancement.

If there is no time designated or preserved for provocative thinking, it is unlikely to occur—as people don't see the forest for the trees when they are in it.

We see some of the most successful leaders employing innovation as a way of doing business, which differentiates them. Are you?

A Remarkable Company Hears the Voice of the Customer

No business leader wakes up every morning and dreams of building an average company. No one hopes that their customer service is under-whelming and that their employees will be uninspired to do their best. Yet, often a chasm exists between wanting and doing.

How do you become a remarkable company? It starts and ends with your customers.

Some of the work that we enjoy most is conducting customer satisfaction surveys. It can be difficult, however, for businesses to receive feedback from their customers, as it may be feedback they may not want to hear. We help business owners and leaders who are courageous enough to test their thinking and assumptions regarding what their customers truly believe, experience, and value.

The objectives are simple and straightforward:

- to find out how the business is perceived in the market
- to learn what else the business can do to better serve customers
- to develop approaches to fill the gaps in customer needs, interests, and expectations

For the businesses we work with, this leads to reinvention of their businesses products, services, or delivery, which leads to growth and sustainability.

Because knowing more about the customer is not always easy to hear and can cause change, we often see companies failing to engage their customers. When companies don't seriously explore customer feedback and perceptions, they miss an important opportunity to grow. Too often leaders focus growth strategies only on their internal beliefs and assumptions about customer satisfaction and needs. While internal assessments are helpful to anticipate customer satisfaction, the only person who can honestly tell you what the customer believes is the customer. As long as you are willing to listen and to act on what you hear, hearing the voice of the customer represents a growth strategy. And responding to what the customer is asking for can make you remarkable.

So, do you really know your customers' perception and level of satisfaction with your business?

Now before you answer, think about this metaphor: the word "customer" represents a coin, and coins have two sides. It's easy to think of your customers as representing a coin—right? (Cha-Ching!). But the customer we are talking about here represents only one of your two customers—the external customer. The other side represents your internal customers—your employees. To become a remarkable company, you must know, understand, and respond to both sides of the coin:

1. Client satisfaction—how your clients and customers experience satisfaction with your company, products, and services, *as delivered by your employees.*
2. Employee satisfaction—that is, how your employees perceive the company and experience working for the company, and what their resulting satisfaction is.

What customer satisfaction means to you, personally, or to your management team, doesn't trump "what is" in the eyes of the customers—your external *and* internal customers.

So if your journey is to become remarkable, then start by understanding your customers, and then prioritize what actions to take based on what you've learned. In business terms, asking your external customer provides you information on your brand perception in the market, and asking your internal customers (employees) provides you with information on your company's culture. Brand is the promise you make to the market; culture is how you deliver on that promise. If you miss one, you miss remarkable.

To do this, that is to become remarkable, requires "backbone." It requires courage, as you will test your thinking, assumptions, and hopes regarding what your customers truly believe and value about you.

Do you know, specifically, what your clients believe and say about you? Effective client survey instruments include questions about your company's behavior:

- communication
- responsiveness
- quality of work and people
- timeliness in delivery
- resource management
- perceived value

And, at the end of the day, what you really need to know about your clients and external customers and how you need to respond to them is four things:

1. Point of Entry – How did they get to you?
2. Overall satisfaction with your products and services
3. Your Net Promoter Score (NPS) – that is, a client's likelihood to recommend or refer your company to colleagues, friends, and family
4. What your customer would like you to do differently or additionally to better meet their needs

Effective climate survey instruments (employee surveys) show what your employees think about working for the company:

- mission, vision, and values
- company direction
- communication
- culture
- retention (loyalty)
- opportunities for growth and development
- leadership perception
- rewards and recognition

Conducting a customer satisfaction program is a differentiator. Its overarching purpose is to help you stay close to your clients, which will help you build upon your clients' satisfaction and loyalty. And there is a long list of benefits inherent to the process. It helps you

- ensure regular touch points with your clients;
- drive industry measurements;
- build and strengthen your client relationships;
- better manage project methodology and delivery efficiency;
- foster quicker course correction;
- better monitor the performance, talent, and leadership of your people (important for leadership and succession development and talent management);
- continually build your client outcomes portfolio (work examples and endorsements).

Employee satisfaction surveys, the flip side of the coin, are similar. These are focused on building a remarkable company to attract, retain, and grow great talent. Questions we use, as outlined above, have parallel survey elements to the external customer survey. However, these questions focus on the internal perception of the company, based on its management and the environment that creates and drives the company's outcomes.

So, how close are you to your customers? What have you done to know their answers to the above questions (as opposed to what you think they are)? Next, what are you doing about that knowledge to make you remarkable?

SUCCESSION READINESS FOR BUSINESS GROWTH AND CONTINUITY

Does your organization have a succession program in place? If it doesn't, don't fret, but do take action. Too many companies and small businesses default to the practice of reactionary assignment of a successor amid a now glaring and vacant position or embark on a swift external hire that often ends up as a high-cost "hiring misfire." The consequences are not only costly but also represent a missed opportunity, due to lack of focus and the inability to support fast growth.

Marshal Goldsmith proposed that succession planning should be called "succession development" (HBR Blog Network, May, 12, 2009). We agree, as a great plan is worth nothing if not pursued. As we repeatedly say, talent initiatives—and succession planning, as a key element—are a process, not an event. It should be understood as a long-term investment for organizational success and legacy versus an expense and an item on a checklist.

A succession strategy is about having an identified plan to fill key positions within your organization. A succession program is the process of identifying, developing, and transitioning potential successors for the company's present and future key roles, aligned with the talent and ambition of its current employees.

A common error we see in succession planning is to target only the key executive roles (such as CEO, COO, or CFO). We see this as a significant risk, unless you are a microbusiness. For example, if you are in the construction or transportation industry, a logistics manager may be critical for the success of your business. Having a vacancy in this position could quickly result in a decrease in service and an increase in customer complaints, and possibly a decrease in customer retention, which is why critical positions across the business need to be identified and replacement processes planned.

COMMON ARGUMENTS AND JUSTIFICATIONS

In our work with companies, we often see that the president or key executive doesn't believe there is an immediate need for a succession plan. The leaders' stated arguments are "We're too small," "We're too new," "We already have good people in place," or "I'm not going anywhere soon." In (an unlikely) static environment where no one leaves, no one gets sick or dies (including the owner or president), growth isn't that important, and performance is exceptional, these arguments may hold true. But the reality is that we don't live in a static business environment. People do leave; they do get sick; they die; the president needs to grow the business; the employees are not all good performers; and some roles are hard to fill.

There is also a tendency to hold on to marginal performers because there is no clear plan on how to replace them. The impact is that the business suffers, the executives suffer, employee morale and productivity decrease, and the customers become less than satisfied with service. And if customers have other options, they'll begin to take them.

Another argument we hear is that small businesses do not have the internal talent pool or a large number of employees to choose from when there is a need to either fill a vacancy or identify an employee to lead a growth initiative. While this is a reality for many small businesses, it does not have to be your destiny.

Business plans are filled with hopes and dreams of rapid growth. Yet, they use a lean-on-the-people strategy to support that growth. This is one reason why business plans fail to meet expectations. It is simply unrealistic to assume that businesses can grow and thrive without a clear plan on how to identify, develop, and place people in critical positions to support growth. It has often been said you cannot grow by cutting. And similarly, you cannot sustain your business (for long) with a gap (talent shortage) that endangers the delivery of your promise to your customers.

Four Key Questions to Help You Assess Your Company's Success Readiness

1. Do you have a people-related plan to support your growth initiatives?
2. Do you have current and relevant job descriptions to establish expectations, role clarity, and accountability of your workforce/talent?
3. Do you have an identified talent pipeline (candidates by talent areas and key positions)?
4. Do you have a process in place for identifying and developing those high-potential, "promising" employees who fill the talent pipeline?

If you do not have the above elements in place, they become challenges and result in

- knee-jerk replacements—either unsuitable hires or "not ready for prime time" promotions that end poorly due to lack of suitability, development, and transition support;
- retention challenges—the best talent leaves to pursue growth and other opportunities, as they do not sense an opportunity at your company to advance in alignment with their career aspirations;
- unnecessary costs in crisis recruiting and training;
- disruption to the work culture/environment, meaning that a sense of stress, discord, competition, and posturing for the position will manifest in employees and could embed in your culture;
- nonexistent or poor "bench strength" to deliver, let alone grow.
  - o Bench strength is a sports analogy used to describe who is available to do the work if the person currently doing it for some reason cannot or is no longer doing it.

A Note on Rightsizing and Succession Planning

Every business owner/executive should spend time on proactively "rightsizing" the company. Unfortunately, rightsizing, over the years, has taken on a negative connotation. It's often seen as a euphemism for firing people. Appropriate rightsizing is simply matching the work force to the workload so that the business is supported and grows in a cost-effective manner. It is because a business is *not* rightsized that it can find itself in the position in which it needs to rightsize for economic reasons.

An up-to-date and well-managed succession plan is a prerequisite to rightsizing your company and supporting growth. We see it as a key leadership initiative and responsibility to and for your organization.

Building a succession program is like any other business program. It has two components: strategy and implementation.

Building Your Strategy

1. The first step in succession readiness is to recognize and accept that the responsibility for it must sit with the top executive as part of his or her job description and performance review. Many organizations with effective succession programs include this metric for all their key executives.

2. The executive team or designated committee needs to explicitly identify current and future *key roles and core talent areas* that are needed to run the company and to support growth initiatives. This includes
   a. identifying an interim process if there is an emergency absence of a key position; and
   b. anticipating future growth and the required talent needed to support it. This will also help you align your recruiting efforts by focusing on interviewing candidates for growth potential and adaptability to address and support the future growth needs of the organization.

IMPLEMENTING YOUR PLAN

1. Management needs to gather information and track high-potential employees. This includes not only their performance in their current roles, but also their commitment to the organization and their career growth ambition. There is a risk that high-potential employees will leave, as they are the quickest to explore and pursue something better. They are also very attractive to your competitors. While seemingly obvious, but unfortunately frequently overlooked, management must practice quality employee performance reviews in order to learn, gather, and track information on the potential successor candidates (also known as maintaining the talent pool or pipeline).

2. The organization will need either to develop or adopt existing methods, tools, and techniques to identify employee competencies and aspirations, such as using talent management systems, talent assessments, or business personality and performance indicators as a means to further assess and develop candidates. This can be done quite efficiently and accurately through candidate feedback and electronic assessments.

3. After assessing and capturing employee capabilities, competencies, and aspirations, you need to implement a structure and process for developing potential successors. Progressive organizations often have formal "emerging leaders" programs.

4. At the point your internal candidates are promoted, we recommend a three- to six-month (minimum) active mentoring and/or coaching process to best transition successors into their new roles.

5. Last, it is important to review and evaluate your succession program's effectiveness annually and update it as required. Consider measurements like number of promotions, employee retention, number of projects successfully performed, and reduced recruiting costs in reviewing the effectiveness of your succession program.

Four Tips to Help You Identify and Develop Your Talent Pool and Potential Successors

1. Keep a finger on the pulse of the talent network in your industry. Talent may be enticed to join your organization based on the opportunities you provide to grow and advance.

2. Develop and maintain a learning organization by integrating regular formal and informal training and skills development to promote a *growth mind-set* among employees (i.e., targeted courses, seminars, workshops, conferences, professional association-sponsored programs, e-learning, in-house brown-bag lunch meetings, peer group exchanges, etc.)

3. Entrench the practice of management delegation above micromanagement. Make sure to give assignments that require the demonstration of skills (enable the candidate to learn new skills) that will be required by managers in your company. (It is important for the candidate to have an opportunity to make and "live" with his or her recommendations.)

4. Make sure your performance review and appraisal system is more than a once-a-year monologue. Conduct at least semiannual reviews to stay in touch with the candidate's performance. And remember, more frequent and informal conversations on progress and performance is more comfortable, meaningful, and supportive of early course correction in your employees. And, if done sincerely and effectively, the review will build trust and your relationship.

   Performance appraisal processes can also include selective 360-degree reviews to focus on skills learned, skills demonstrated, skills to be learned, what went well, what can be done better, professional and career goals, and how colleagues see the candidate's performance and behavior.

While often overlooked or misunderstood, succession planning is an important component for business growth and organizational sustainability and success. Whether you have a formal plan or an informal plan is less important than that you have a plan and you work on it throughout the year. Business growth needs people to support it. Defining who you need now and in the future and who will replace key positions is an important and necessary growth strategy. The right talent in the right area will carry you forward and will manifest in the success of your business strategy.

WHY START YOUR EXIT PLANNING NOW?

How much time do you spend thinking about exit planning? If you're like many of the small business owners we meet—not much. That's okay, as long as you don't care about supporting yourself and your family when you retire, and you are not attached to what happens to the business, your employees, and your customers after you leave. But in truth, the business people we meet do care. They care a lot—they just haven't done much about it yet.

In the previous section, we described the importance of succession planning development. We focused primarily on supporting business growth. But business growth, for you, also has a positive end point: exiting the business in a way that provides for your retirement. And just like you need to have a succession plan, you, personally, need to think about your exit plan.

Unfortunately, many business owners we encounter believe that their business will just dissolve when they exit and don't believe or understand that their business could have value and be sold. Some business owners are counting on their business to help support their retirement, yet have done nothing to position their business so it can do so.

In developing your exit plan (or to understand better why an exit plan is important for you right now), it is necessary to understand the two key reasons businesses have value and the three types of exits.

Two reasons your business can have value:

1. To grow the acquirer's business
    a. by adding a new service or product line
    b. by enhancing an existing service/product line through the addition of your company
2. To remove you as a competitor!

Three types of exits:

1. Involuntary—meaning your business stops growing, and you go out of business
2. Unexpected—due to death, illness, or disability
3. Voluntary—retirement or proactive selling opportunity

And here's why exit planning (including buy-sell-transfer agreements) is critical for you earlier than later: An exit plan better prepares you (the business owner) for the inevitable transition of your business—whether it's expected (intended) or unexpected (the result of undesirable circumstances that can and do arise).

Most business owners we talk to understand the voluntary exit (even if they are not currently planning for it). And they also understand—or perhaps a better word is *fear*—an involuntary exit. What is less discussed is the unexpected exit.

An unexpected exit may be triggered by a biological event, what we have coined "the biology of exit planning." A biological event can be

- you die;
- you become ill or disabled;
- you're too old to effectively run the business.

Biological events are seldom discussed, yet are a looming reality in business life. And due to the sensitivity of the topic, many people simply avoid addressing them in their exit planning, and then employees are left to deal with the muddle of unknowns amid the highly emotional and sometimes financial losses of an owner.

Regardless of whether the exit event is planned (such as the sale of the company or leadership succession of an employee or family member) or not (a biological event), at some point there will be a transition.

So we ask again, how much time have you spent thinking about and formulating an exit plan that considers not only the planned exit options, but also the unplanned exit possibilities?

We suggest you start with one key question:

Can your business continue if you could no longer run it tomorrow?

If the answer is *yes—absolutely*, then you are well-prepared for a sale or for a biological event. If your answer is no, because the business relies either solely or primarily on you for sales and key operational activities, you are not a very attractive acquisition target. And should a biological event occur, sustaining the business will be a serious challenge.

Clearly, we recommend that regardless of where you are in your business life cycle (whether it's a start-up or nearing the end of your tenure), you have an exit plan. You now may appreciate why you need to work on your business to prepare it to achieve your personal objectives when you leave. And an added benefit—as you continue to work on your business, it will gain in value.

If you are still not completely convinced that you need an exit plan, then we ask you to do the following exercise to determine how well-positioned you are for leaving the company, either willfully or by elements outside of your control.

Set aside some time and answer the following questions:

1. Where do you see yourself in three to five years?
   a. retired
   b. still working with the company
   c. sold the company, and either started a new company or are working for another company

2. When do you plan to retire?
   a. be specific
   b. if you say, "I will never retire," remember the reality of biological events

3. What is the income you will need when you retire to maintain your current (or an acceptable) lifestyle?
   a. working with your accountant or financial advisor, answer these questions:

    i.   what are your current expenses?

    ii. what will your expenses be upon retirement?

    iii. what are your current assets? (savings, investments, whole-life insurance, property, other)

    iv. what other income streams are available to you upon retirement? (Social Security, spouse's pension, pension you may have from a previous employer, other)

    v. how much is needed from your business to support your retirement? (We call this filling in the gap.)

4. What do you expect from the company to support your retirement? (This amount could be from a sale or from an ongoing financial payment, possibly as part of a buy-out.)
   a. how much money per year? Be specific.
   b. how many years?

5. What needs to happen with the company to support your retirement objective?

Question five is a key question if there is an expectation that the business will provide funds to you after you retire. Question five begins the thoughtful and planned process for exiting the business. It is the exit plan, and it is based on your expectations and what will be required for the business to support your post-business goals.

While formulating an exit plan will require some "frontloading" in time, the benefits of your effort will pay off by

- allowing you to control and better manage your exit;
- helping you to maximize the company's value;
- minimizing tax implications;
- establishing multiple exit options, which mitigates the unknowns and negative unexpected circumstances (such as serious injury/disability, death, divorce, disagreement/owner deadlock, etc.);

- better enabling you to achieve business and personal goals;
- reducing stress and anxiety due to prior planning and defined expectations;
- ensuring business continuity.

And this means that if you manage a profitable business, have an excellent reputation, and are unique or somewhat unique in your value—the buying price includes goodwill.

To help you best position yourself (and your family) for your exit and to position your business to get what you want from it (its worth or legacy or both), we strongly encourage that the owner(s)/partner(s) start with answering these key questions and then doing what is required to prepare you for your exit.

APPENDIX

ORGANIZATIONAL GRAVITY INVENTORY

A Management Self-Assessment Tool

The Organizational Gravity Inventory self-assessment will enable you to evaluate your business and how it performs based on the organizational gravity model. Your scores will determine where you should focus your growth efforts.

Section I: Company Information

Company Name:

Years in Business:

Revenue:

Revenue Growth YoY %:

Contribution Margin %:

Contribution Margin Improvement YoY %:

Net Income %:

Net Income Improvement YoY %

Number of Employees:
- Full-time:
- Part-time:
- Subcontractors (1099):
- Temps:

Turnover:
Number of people leaving and how long each person was with the company

Comments/Observations:

	Section II: Assessment Elements					
The rating scale is from 1 to 4, with 1 being "no, we don't do this," and 4 being "yes, we do this very well." In each category, rate your success and effectiveness in achieving the stated goals.						
No.	Question	1	2	3	4	Comments
Organizational Structure						
1	Rate the quality and completeness of your organizational chart					
Strategy						
2	Creating a direction/ vision for the next 12–36 months					
3	Creating a mission or purpose statement					
4	Pursuing stated, written, and practiced company values that successfully guide your culture and align how you and your employees work together					
5	Reaching your goals					
6	Implementing strategic initiatives					
7	Basing important business decisions on evidence and analytics					
8	Successfully aligning your executive team around your strategy, mission, vision, and values					

No.	Question	1	2	3	4	Comments
Branding						
9	Actively promoting the image you want prospects and clients to have of your business.					
10	Articulating your competitive advantage and differentiating your business from your competitors					
11	Clearly identifying your niche market to your team					
12	Selling to your target market					
13	Clearly articulating your brand promise on key marketing elements: website, social media, collateral					
14	Presenting your brand message clearly and consistently across all communication channels (internal and external)					
15	Developing a broad social media presence?					
15.1	- LinkedIn					
15.2	- Facebook or Google+					

No.	Question	1	2	3	4	Comments
15.3	- Twitter					
15.4	- YouTube					
16	Successfully reflecting your business, what it does, and its value proposition on your website					
17	Effectively soliciting and receiving client feedback					
18	Taking action at least every six months on client feedback					
19	Maintaining a sales pipeline and/or using a CRM system (if applicable)					
Culture						
20	Delivering on your brand promise					
21	Ensuring that you and your employees can accurately describe the culture of your organization					
22	Writing and distributing an operational guide or policy-and-procedures manual					

No.	Question	1	2	3	4	Comments
23	Developing a communications system to provide employees with the information necessary to perform their roles optimally					
24	Maintaining an employee handbook that is current and relevant?					
25	Receiving and evaluating feedback on employee opinions and satisfaction					
26	Preparing daily, weekly, or monthly automated reports to show how your business is doing on key performance indicators					
27	Completing standard monthly financial reports to track the financial health of your business and help drive decisions?					
27.1	- Balance Sheet					
27.2	- Profit-and-Loss Statement					
27.3	- Cash Flow					
27.4	- Aged A/R					

No.	Question	1	2	3	4	Comments
Talent Management						
28	Acquiring the talent to deliver on your brand promise					
29	Acquiring the talent to *grow* your business					
30	Establishing effective hiring and recruitment practices					
31	Developing clear and relevant role definitions and job/position descriptions					
32	Successfully integrating employees into the company and their job roles					
33	Implementing an effective and reliable employee performance appraisal/evaluation system					
34	Offering an employee incentives, rewards, and recognition program					
35	Understanding why people choose to work for you?					

No.	Question	1	2	3	4	Comments
36	Understanding why employees leave					
37	Developing a plan to overcome potential harm to your business if key employees leave					
38	Creating a succession plan to reduce risk and ensure continuity in key/pivotal positions in the company					
39	Developing a management or leadership program to support business growth and the next generation of leaders					
40	Determining if employees are satisfied and engaged					
41	Determining if employees are performing to your satisfaction					
Exit Planning						
42	Preparing and updating an exit plan					

We invite you to share your inventory with us for a confidential, courtesy consultation regarding your questions our recommendations to focus your efforts to grow your business. Scan your completed inventory and email to: Info@ KubicaLaForestConsulting.com or call us at 401 885 2011 (RI Office) or 805 904 6450 (CA office).

References and Notes

Introduction

1. Throughout the book we will use the terms *organizational gravity* and *gravitational organization* interchangeably.
2. Pruitt, B. (2011, September 29). High-growth entrepreneurs plan to continue growing [Press release]. Retrieved March 1, 2013, from http://www.kauffman.org/newsroom/high-growth-entrepreneurs-plan-to-continue-growing.aspx
3. *Talent shortage 2011 survey results* [Pamphlet; PDF]. (2011). Retrieved from http://us.manpower.com/us/en/multimedia/2011-Talent-Shortage-Survey.pdf

Chapter 1 Business Growth Strategy

1. Rumelt, R. (2011). *Good strategy/bad strategy*. New York: Crown Business.

Chapter 2 Business Growth Strategy Supplement: A Series of Tips and Techniques to Help with Strategy Formulation and Guidance

1. Lublin, J. S., & Mattioli, D. (2010, January 25). Strategic plans lose favor. *The Wall Street Journal*. Retrieved from http://online.wsj.com/article/SB100014240527487038 22404575019283591121478.html
2. Carroll, L. (2009). *Alice's adventures in Wonderland* (2009 ed.). New York: Oxford University Press.
3. In the beginning – let there be shoes. (n.d.). Retrieved March 1, 2013, from http://about.zappos.com/zappos-story/ in-the-beginning-let-there-be-shoes
4. Zappos family core values. (n.d.). Retrieved March 1, 2013, from http://about.zappos.com/our-unique-culture/ zappos-core-values/
5. Rumelt, *ibid*.
6. Leinwand, P., & Mainardi, C. (2010, December 15). Why can't Kmart be successful while Target and Walmart thrive [Blog post]. Retrieved from http://blogs.hbr.org/ cs/2010/12/why_cant_kmart_be_successful_w.html
7. Maher, K. (2011, August 10). At Indiana machine shop, tough calls amid turmoil. *The Wall Street Journal*, Management. Retrieved from http://online.wsj.com/arti-cle/SB100014240531119044809045764986014538646 90.html
8. Pfeffer, J., & Sutton, R. I. (2006). *Hard facts, dangerous half-truths and total nonsense: Profiting from evidence-based management*. Harvard Business School Press.
9. Grove, A. S. (1999). *Only the paranoid survive: How to exploit the crisis points that challenge every company*. New York: Currency.

10. Goltz, J. (2011, January 5). Top 10 reasons small businesses fail. *The New York Times*, Business Day. Retrieved from http://boss.blogs.nytimes.com/2011/01/05/top-10-reasons-small-businesses-fail/

11. Suess, D. (1973). *Did I ever tell you how lucky you are?* New York: Random House.

12. Wasserman, N. (2012). *The founder's dilemma: Anticipating and avoiding the pitfalls that can sink a startup.* Princeton University Press.

13. Pfeffer, J., & Sutton, R. I. (2000). *The knowing-doing gap.* Harvard Business School Press.

Chapter 3 Branding

1. Ulanoff, L. (2011, December 20). 2011: Tech's biggest winners and losers. Retrieved March 4, 2013, from http://mashable.com/2011/12/20/tech-winners-losers-2011/

2. Kim, S., & Gutman, M. (Writers). (2011, November 1). Bank of America cancels $5 fee [Television webisode]. In *ABC World News with Diane Sawyer*. Retrieved from http://abcnews.go.com/Business/bank-america-drops-plan-debit-card-fee/story?id=14857970#.UEflQaRrO5M

3. Wagstaff, K. (2011, October 24). Netflix loses 800,000 subscribers after price hike, Qwikster debacle. Time. Retrieved from http://techland.time.com/2011/10/24/netflix-loses-800000-subscribers-after-price-hike-qwikster-debacle/

4. Epstein, Z. (2012, July 2). Apple's smartphone OS share hits all-time high in June, Blackberry dips below 2%. Retrieved March 4, 2013, from http://bgr.com/2012/07/02/iphone-market-share-june-2012-android-blackberry

5. McIntyre, D. A. (2012, June 21). 10 brands that will disappear in 2013. Retrieved March 4, 2013, from 24/7 Wall St. website: http://finance.yahoo.com/news/10-brands-that-will-disappear-in-2013.html?page=all

6. Sullivan, J., Ph.D. (December 5, 2005) A case Study of Google Recruiting. Retrieved from http://www.ere. net/2005/12/05/a-case-study-of-google-recruiting/

7. Recruitment strategy and competitive position on the job market. (n.d.). Retrieved March 4, 2013, from *HR Management Guide* website: http://www.simplehrguide. com/recruitment-strategy-and-competitive-position-on-the-job-market.html

Chapter 4 Branding Companion Chapter—Examples, Tips and Techniques

1. Scott, D. M. (2010). *New rules of marketing and PR: How to use social media, blogs, news releases, online video, and viral marketing to reach buyers directly.* Hoboken, NJ: John Wiley & Sons.

Chapter 6 Culture Companion Chapter—Examples, Tips and Techniques

1. Logan, D., King, J., & Fischer-Wright, H. (2011). *Tribal leadership: Leveraging natural groups to build a thriving organization.* New York: Harper Business.

2. Stefanovich, A. (2011). *Look at more: The proven approach to innovation growth and change.* San Francisco: Jossey-Bass.

3. Godin, S. (2008). *Tribes:* We need you to lead us. New York: Portfolio.

Chapter 7 Progressive Talent Management

1. Gostick, A., & Elton, C. (2009). *The carrot principle: How the best managers use recognition to engage their people, retain talent, and accelerate performance* (April 2009 ed.). New York: Free Press.

2. Jackson, E. (2011, December 14). Top ten reasons why large companies fail to keep their best talent.

Forbes. Retrieved from http://www.forbes.com/sites/ ericjackson/2011/12/14/

Chapter 8 Talent Development and Management Companion Chapter

1. Watkins, M. (2003). *The first 90 days: Critical success strategies for new leaders at all levels.* Harvard Business School Press.
2. *Ibid.*
3. Watkins, M. (2009). *Your Next Move: The leader's guide to navigating career transitions.* Harvard Business Press.

Bonus Section (Leadership)

1. Doltich, D. L., Ph.D., & Cairo, P. C., Ph.D. (2003). *Why CEOs fail: The 11 behaviors that can derail your climb to the top and how to manage them.* San Francisco: Jossey-Bass.
2. Goldsmith, M., & Reiter, M. (2007). *What Got You Here Won't Get You There: How successful people become even more successful.* New York: Hyperion.

ACKNOWLEDGEMENTS

From Tony

Writing a book like this is never done alone. And it is through the thoughtful support of others that the product begins to have definition and take shape. I first want to thank my co-author, Sara. Without her this project would not have happened. She has been the motivating force since day one. Also, my son Jeremy who provided thoughtful guidance as the project developed. To my other son Rob who sat with me in the backyard listening as I droned on about the ideas and concepts presented in this book. And to my daughter Neysa who would say to me time and time again as I was getting discouraged, "Dad this is something you've wanted to do for a long time—just keep going." Ryan McCarthy, a dear friend, provided a perspective from the users' point of view that helped move the book in a more complete direction. To Michael Kubica who was the eyes behind the words. Not only did he do an excellent job editing, but he also asked thoughtful questions throughout. And finally to my wife Edie, who had to put up with endless hours writing, being late more times than I want to admit, and listening to me whine about writer's block. Her continuing and loving support is so important. Thank you.

From Sara

In acknowledgment and appreciation of my dear business partner, friend and colleague, Tony Kubica, without whom I would not be where I am today. With gratitude to the Kubica family members who are so welcoming to me, and supportive of our work and KLC. Thank you Edith, Rob (and Hannah), Neysa (and Bob and Molly), Jeremy, Michael, and Ryan McCarthy. What a truly lovely group of people you are.

With heartfelt joy and gratitude for the love and endless support I receive from my husband, Andrew, my mother, Ruth Young, and my sister, Kelly Bowen. You fill my world with abundance.

To our very talented and dedicated clients and colleagues, we are privileged to work with you and to support your growth – thank you. It's a grand journey.

Lastly, in appreciation of those who have mentored me and promoted my professional growth and development over the years, thank you...may I do the same for those emerging who are driven to advance their careers and grow their businesses.

COMPANY BIOGRAPHY

KUBICA ▲ LAFOREST
CONSULTING

Sara LaForest

Tony Kubica

www.KubicaLaForestConsulting.com

Tony Kubica and Sara LaForest, Partners of Kubica LaForest Consulting, are Business Growth Advisors, Executive/ Performance Coaches, Speakers, and Authors.

Kubica LaForest Consulting specializes in a high touch, personalized approach in helping entrepreneurs and executives of global companies and organizations improve their business performance and accelerate their business growth.

They specialize in understanding the organizational and people factors in getting work done and growing businesses. They help business owners and organizational leaders Build Remarkable Companies through Strategy and Business Growth Initiatives, Brand-Building for market differentiation, Organizational Alignment and Culture Building, Talent and Leadership Development, and they provide support for key transitions such as new manager integration, emerging leaders, and succession planning and exit readiness.

In addition to their consulting, coaching and organizational development work, they are widely published internationally and train and speak at conferences and events across the country. As featured authors, their work has been published in *Leadership Excellence, Sales and Service Excellence, Personal Excellence, Healthcare Executive, Foxbusiness.com, (CEO)refresher. com, Leader-values.com, Providence Business News, Women Entrepreneur, WE Magazine for Women, Evan Carmichael. com, CNN.com, PerformanceXpress.org, Customerservice. com, MicroSoftDynamics.com, ERE.Net, Exitplanninginstitute. org, smallbusinessonlinecommunity.bankofamerica.com, Expertaccess.sycom.com, Startupnation.com, Getentreprenuer. com, Customerthink.com, Alaska Business Magazine, CEOworld. biz,* and many others.

Professional affiliations include the Institute of Management Consultants (IMC), American Management Association (AMAnet), and the Center for Creative Leadership (CCL). They also hold certification with Hogan Assessment Systems.

For additional free information on organizational gravity, business growth, and related topics and to learn more about their services go to http://www.kubicalaforestconsulting.com and their blog http://yourbusinessgyroscope.com.

We welcome you to contact us directly at:
Tony@KubicaLaForestConsulting.com and
Sara@KubicaLaForestConsulting.com.